YOUTH ED

THE
CASE
FOR
CHRIST

Resources by Lee Strobel

The Case for Christ
The Case for Christ audio
The Case for Christ—Youth Edition (with Jane Vogel)
The Case for Faith
The Case for Faith audio
God's Outrageous Claims
Inside the Mind of Unchurched Harry and Mary
What Jesus Would Say

YOUTH EDITION

THE CASE FOR CHRIST

A journalist's personal investigation of the evidence for Jesus

LEE STROBEL

WITH JANE VOGEL

ZONDERVAN®

ZONDERVAN.com/
AUTHORTRACKER
follow your favorite authors

www.invertbooks.com

 **ZONDERVAN®**

The Case for Christ — Youth Edition
Copyright © 2001 by Lee Strobel
International Trade Paper Edition

Requests for information should be addressed to:

Zondervan, Grand Rapids, Michigan 49530

ISBN-10: 0-310-24219-3
ISBN-13: 978-0-310-24219-2

Interior design by Todd Sprague

Printed in the United States of America

07 08 09 10 11 12 • 15 14 13 12 11 10 9

CONTENTS

Introduction

My friends and I were celebrating at an Italian restaurant across the street from the University of Missouri. I was set to graduate in a few days, and I had just accepted a job offer: a three-month internship at the *Chicago Tribune,* with a promise that if I performed well, I'd get a permanent job as a reporter.

At one point during the meal, somewhere between the bread sticks and the Neapolitan ice cream, my best friend, Ersin, made an offhand remark about how my internship was certainly a great gift from God.

His comment startled me. During the four years I'd known Ersin, I don't think we'd ever talked about religion.

"Wait a minute, let me get this straight," I said. "Are you telling me that someone as intelligent as you—valedictorian, science whiz, and all that—

that you actually believe that God exists? I always figured you were beyond that!"

It was clear that Ersin was equally surprised. "What are you trying to tell *me?*" he said. "Are you saying there *isn't* a God? Are you telling me that someone as intelligent as you *doesn't* believe in God? You've got to be kidding!"

We were both genuinely astonished. I couldn't believe that a sharp person like Ersin had actually bought into a fairy tale like the existence of an all-powerful, all-knowing Creator of the universe. Hadn't he learned anything at college?

If you could freeze-frame my attitude toward God, that would be it: Intelligent people didn't believe in him. All it took was a quick look at the evidence to know that Christianity was nothing but superstition and wishful thinking.

But to be honest, that's all I had ever really given the evidence: a quick look. And I was happy to keep it that way for years—until one day, my life took a strange turn, pushing me into an all-out investigation into the facts surrounding the case for Christianity.

That's what this book is about. I'll take you along as I retrace the events that led to a nearly 2-year exploration of the evidence for and against believing in Christ.

After weighing the evidence, I made my decision. But I can't make yours. That's your choice. I hope you take it seriously, because there may be more at stake than just idle curiosity. If Jesus is to be believed—and I realize that may be a big *if* for you at this point—then nothing is more important than how you respond to him.

Check out the evidence for yourself.

What's Wrong with Me?

I could take you back to the very place where I lost my faith in God. I was 14 years old.

At Prospect High School in Mount Prospect, Illinois, the biology classroom was on the third floor in the northwest corner of the building. I was sitting in the second row from the windows, third chair from the front, when I first learned about Darwin's theory of evolution.

REVOLUTIONIZED BY EVOLUTION

This was revolutionary to me! Our teacher explained that life originated millions of years ago when chemicals randomly reacted with each other in a warm ocean on the primordial earth. Then, through a process of survival of the fittest and natural selection, life forms gained in complexity.

Eventually, human beings emerged from the same family tree as apes.

Although the teacher didn't address this aspect of evolution, its biggest implication was obvious to me: If evolution explains the origin and development of life, then God was out of a job! What did we need God for? Life was just the natural result of the random interaction of chemicals.

To my mind, this was great news! Finally, here was a rational basis for atheism. If evolution explains life, then the first chapters of the Bible must be mythology or wishful thinking. And if that were true of the first chapters, why not the rest? Jesus could not have been God. Miracles aren't possible; they're just the attempts by pre-scientific people to make sense out of what they couldn't understand but which now science can explain.

For the first time, I had a rational reason to abandon Christianity.

BORED BY RELIGION

Not that I'd ever really been a Christian.

My parents believed in God and had done their best to try to spark spiritual interest in me. When I was a kid, they brought me to a Protestant church, where I would struggle to stay awake during the 20-minute sermons. I didn't understand the rituals, I couldn't relate to the organ music, and I quickly concluded that religion was a waste of an otherwise perfectly good Sunday.

When I was in junior high, my parents enrolled me in confirmation class. This meant that one day a week after school I was forced to sit in the church's airless basement and go through a series of classes.

I can't recall learning much about the Bible—or about Jesus, for that matter. Mostly, I remember having to memorize things like the Ten Commandments and then stand and recite them. Nobody knew them well; we sort of bluffed our way through as the pastor would prompt us. It was mind-numbingly dull. I don't remember anything that I was forced to commit to memory back then, although I do have vivid memories of the pastor lecturing us and telling us sternly that we didn't have enough "diligence." I didn't even know what that was, but apparently we were bad for not having it.

GRADUATING FROM CHURCH

When the time came to be formally confirmed and made a member of the church, we were told in advance the kind of questions we would be asked so that we'd know the answers. I didn't want to go through with this because, if I had *any* faith in God at the time, it was hanging by a slender thread. To me, God was irrelevant, mysterious, and a stern disciplinarian who, if he existed, was probably mad that I lacked "diligence."

On the other hand, I wasn't too excited about the idea of standing up to my parents and saying, "No thanks, I'm not interested in being confirmed, because I think your God is probably just a fairy tale." My dad would have gone ballistic and my mom would have freaked out. I didn't need that. If there were no God, then what would be the harm in going through some meaningless ritual?

So I went through the confirmation ceremony. Afterward, we got a stack of pre-printed envelopes so we could give money to the church. That, I figured, was probably what was really behind the whole confirmation scam—and probably behind all of organized religion. But confirmation had its advantages: I figured that my confirmation ceremony was actually my graduation ceremony—I had graduated from church. Now I was on my own. My parents stopped dragging me to church on Sundays, and I was happy to sleep late. I had done the religion drill. Time to party!

LOOKING FOR LOVE

After that day in biology class, I had even more reason to party. After all, I'd figured out that God did not exist. And that meant I was not accountable to him. I would not have to stand before him someday and be judged. I was free to live according to *my* rules, not his dusty commandments that I had been force-fed in confirmation class. To me, all of this meant that nobody else really mattered unless they made me happy.

But there *was* someone who mattered—and who made me happy. Her name was Leslie, and we met when we were 14 years old. On the day we met, Leslie went home and told her mother, "I've met the boy I'm going to marry!"

Her mother was condescending. "Sure, you did," she said. But Leslie didn't have any doubts, and neither did I.

We dated on and off during high school, and after I left home to attend the University of Missouri, we maintained our relationship through the mail. We became convinced that there was nobody else we would ever be happy with. Within a year, Leslie moved down to Missouri, and we got engaged. We decided to get married in a church because. . .well, that's where people get married, isn't it?

Besides, Leslie wasn't hostile toward God, as I was. She wasn't opposed to religion, especially for other people. For herself, though, God was just another topic she had never taken the time to seriously explore.

LIVING IN HIGH GEAR

After I finished college, we moved to a high-rise apartment not far from Tribune Tower in downtown Chicago. Leslie was busy with her banking career. I was beginning to climb the ladder at the *Chicago Tribune,* where my internship had led to a permanent job as a reporter.

That's when my life power-shifted into high gear. If I had a god at that time, it was my career. I loved seeing my name in print, and I thrived on the cutthroat environment, the adrenaline rush of deadlines, and the get-the-story-at-any-cost mentality.

I was doing what I had always dreamed of: traveling around the country; doing radio and TV interview shows; writing a book; winning awards. I had *made* it! I was on the fast track to the top of my profession, and I wasn't even 30 years old.

WHAT'S WRONG WITH ME?

The power I had was better than any high I could get off drugs or alcohol. There were times when I used that power to help people. I remember doing a Thanksgiving Day feature about a poor family on Chicago's West Side. The two young sisters didn't even have a coat, and only one sweater for the two of them. During the biting Chicago winter, one little girl would wear the sweater halfway to school, then the other would wear it the rest of the distance.

After my article appeared, big-hearted people from around the city showered the family with gifts and money. I went back to visit them on Christmas Eve and found their home overflowing with presents—and their closet so stuffed that it looked like the coat department at Nordstrom's. And all, I told myself, because of my article.

But after a while, I noticed that I really didn't care about other people. I once interviewed a grieving woman whose young daughter had been raped and murdered. As she poured out her pain, I was thinking, "Wow! These are great quotes! And I'm the only reporter who's got them!" I didn't care about her daughter or her despair; I was after a front-page byline and another bonus from the boss.

Other people noticed my hardening heart. Once I covered a trial in which a teenager testified how a gang had lined up him, his brother, and a friend against a wall and then, one by one, shot them point-blank in the head. The two others died instantly; somehow, this teenager had survived. At least, he survived long enough to point out the killer in court. According to a doctor's testimony, it was only a matter of time before the witness himself would die from his injuries.

After the trial was over, the prosecutor let me interview the teenager for a feature story. I was excited—I knew I had a front-page exclusive. I was so stoked about beating the competition to the story that I had a big grin on my face as I pumped the kid for information.

In the middle of the interview, the prosecutor pulled me aside and said, angrily, "Strobel, what's wrong with you? This kid watched his brother and his friend get blown away, he's probably going to die himself, and you're interviewing him like you're a comedian or something."

His words haunted me for a long time. What *was* wrong with me? Why didn't I care about that kid or his murdered friends? Why didn't I empathize with the woman whose daughter had been murdered? Why did I only care about myself and my career? And worst of all, why didn't all my success satisfy me? Why did I always want more?

MAN IN THE MIRROR

But it wasn't my secret dissatisfaction that prompted me to look into the claims of Christianity. It was my wife.

Sometimes I hear Christians say that unbelievers can't have a happy marriage because they don't know what true love is. Well, we knew enough about it to be pretty fulfilled. We were best friends, living an exhilarating life, and for the most part didn't have any worries. This is how I picture our life back then: It was as if Leslie and I were driving through life in a convertible sports car, laughing and joking, totally carefree and happy.

So I was stunned when Leslie announced that she had become a Christian. I rolled my eyes and braced for the worst. I felt like the victim of some kind of scam. I had married one Leslie—the fun Leslie, the carefree Leslie, the risk-taking Leslie—and now I was afraid she was going to turn into some sort of sexually repressed prude who would trade our upwardly mobile lifestyle for all-night prayer meetings and volunteer work in grimy soup kitchens.

Instead I was pleasantly surprised—even fascinated—by the changes in her character, her integrity, and her personal confidence. At the same time, the more Leslie changed in positive ways, the more obvious it became that my own life and relationships were messed up. It was as if Leslie were holding up a mirror and I was seeing myself as I really was—and I didn't like the picture.

EXAMINING THE EVIDENCE

What finally brought me to faith in God was truth. I was a journalist. I had legal training from Yale Law School. I knew how to investigate a case and how to sift the evidence. And I knew how to face facts. If the evidence of history established convincingly that Jesus is who he claimed to be—the one-and-only Son of God—then I would have no choice but to follow him. My fruitless pursuit of happiness changed into a relentless pursuit of truth. That's what fueled my investigation into the evidence about Christ.

The rest of this book retraces that investigation. Of course, the questions I asked and the evidence I uncovered didn't always follow a logical, step-by-step progression. I'd look into one aspect of Christianity, then another and another, then maybe return with new questions to the first issue. For 21 months I committed myself to exploring the case for and against Christ with an open mind. And that's all I ask of you: Start with an open mind, and see where the evidence leads you.

WHO IS THIS JESUS?

one

Did Jesus Really Think He Was God?

imagine that one morning as you poured yourself a bowl of Wheaties, a game ticket fell out of the box. Looking at it, you realized that you were the lucky winner of an all-expense-paid vacation to Hawaii!

Now, less than three weeks later, you're suited up and ready to take on the Pacific surf. Since you didn't happen to carry a surfboard with you on the plane, you stroll over to a little rental shack on the beach to check out a board.

Ahead of you in line are two guys trying to explain why they should get their deposits back even though they failed to return their surfboards.

"It was an act of nature, man," says the first guy. "This monster wave came and swept the board right out from under me. By the time I got my head above water, the board was out of sight. By now it's probably halfway to Hong Kong."

Then the second guy offers his excuse. "I didn't lose my board. But just as I was bringing it back, Keanu Reeves stopped me and said he needed it for a stunt in some new action film he's making. I figured it would be good publicity for your surf shop, so I let him have it. I'm sure he'll return it when he's done."

Now, the surf shop clerk, who wasn't born yesterday, knows a scam when he sees one. He figures that these guys have ripped off his boards and have the gall to try to get their deposits back besides. It shouldn't be too hard to check up on the Keanu Reeves story. A few phone calls will reveal whether he's on the island shooting a new movie. If he's not, the customer has been caught in a lie and the shop can prosecute. A runaway wave, now—that's going to be a little harder to confirm or disprove.

When I decided to test the claims of Christianity, right off the bat I figured that Christians had made a tactical error. Other religions believe in all kinds of invisible gods—sort of like the monster wave story—and that's kind of hard to pin down one way or the other. But Christians were basing their religion on the alleged teachings and miracles of someone they claim is an actual historical person—Jesus Christ—who, they say, is God.

This struck me as a major mistake. If Jesus really lived, he would have left behind some historical evidence. I couldn't call him up the way you could phone Keanu Reeves' agent, but if he really lived, then I ought to be able to find *some* information on him. I figured all that I needed to do was dig out the historical truth about Jesus. It would reveal that he was a nice man, maybe a very moral person and excellent teacher—but certainly not a god.

Frankly, I was pretty sure that Jesus himself would agree with me. The real Jesus, I was confident, would roll over in his grave if he knew people were worshiping him. I hadn't really studied Jesus' teachings, but I doubted that he had ever claimed to be anything more than a traveling teacher and an occasional rabble-rouser.

WHO DID JESUS SAY HE WAS?

A lot of the information we have about Jesus comes from the Bible. That's a problem right there, because why should we believe that the Bible is an accurate source of information? So I spent a lot of time investigating the accuracy of the Bible—especially the New Testament, which is where most of the information about Jesus is. Chapters 5 and 6 retrace that investigation.

Whether you believe the Bible is reliable or not, there's no denying that Christians consider the Bible their sourcebook for what they believe about Jesus. I suspected that Christians had misread the whole thing—that other people had made claims for Jesus that Jesus himself would never back up. If I could demonstrate from the Bible itself that Jesus never claimed to be God, then I wouldn't have to go any further.

The gospel of John in the New Testament opens with a majestic claim that Jesus, here called "the Word," is God.

> In the beginning was the Word, and the Word was with God, and the Word was God. He was with God in the beginning. Through him all things were made; without him nothing was made that has been made....The Word became flesh and made his dwelling among us. We have seen his glory, the glory of the One and Only, who came from the Father, full of grace and truth.
>
> John 1:1-3, 14, NIV

As I read those claims (made, you'll notice, by one of Jesus' followers, not by Jesus himself), I wondered how Jesus would respond. Would he say, "Whoa! John got me all wrong?" Or would he nod approvingly and say, "Yep, I'm all that—and more"?

God—if he exists—is supposed to have certain characteristics, also called "attributes." One way of investigating whether Jesus is God is to see how well he measured up to those attributes. Here are some claims the Bible makes about Jesus. Of course, whether you believe those claims depends on whether you believe the Bible. You might want to wait to make up your mind on that until you've read chapters 5 and 6.

Attributes of God	Claims about Jesus
Omniscience (all-knowing)	In John 16:30 the apostle John affirms of Jesus, "Now we can see that you know all things."
Omnipresence (everywhere present)	Jesus said in Matthew 28:20, "Surely I am with you always, to the very end of the age."
Omnipotence (all-powerful)	"All authority in heaven and on earth has been given to me," Jesus said in Matthew 28:18.
Eternality (no beginning or end)	John 1:1 declares of Jesus, "In the beginning was the Word, and the Word was with God, and the Word was God."
Immutability (unchanging)	Hebrews 13:8 says, "Jesus Christ is the same yesterday and today and forever."

"CALL ME CHRIST"

I found one account of what Jesus said about himself in another New Testament book, the gospel of Matthew. In a private meeting, Jesus asked his disciples, "Who do you say I am?" Peter answered, "You're the Christ, the Messiah, the Son of the living God." Jesus' response? "God bless you, Simon, son of Jonah! You didn't get that answer out of books or from teachers. My Father in heaven, God himself, let you in on this secret of who I really am" (Matthew 16:15–17, *THE MESSAGE*).

Although this conversation sounded as if Jesus might be claiming to be more than just the good teacher I'd had him pegged as, I wasn't convinced that the titles "Christ" and even "Son of the living God" necessarily had to be interpreted to mean "God." What did the people around Jesus think he meant when he said he was the Christ?

I found an answer to that question in a short but violent account in the gospel of John. Some of the Jewish leaders gathered around Jesus and said, "How long will you keep us in suspense? If you are the Christ, tell us plainly." Jesus responded, "I did tell you, but you do not believe. . . . I and the Father are one."

While the claim, "I and the Father are one," didn't mean much to me, it clearly meant something very specific to the people listening to Jesus, because at once they picked up rocks to stone him! Why? "For blasphemy," they said, "because you, a mere man, claim to be God." (You can read this conversation in John 10:24–33.)

Some of Jesus' statements as they are recorded in the Bible don't seem to be clear claims that Jesus is God. I thought this might be an argument against the idea that Jesus claimed to be God. For an "expert's" opinion, I asked Dr. Ben Witherington, who has a whole string of degrees and memberships in societies that study the Bible and has written five books about Jesus.

NO CLEAR CLAIMS

To: Ben Witherington
From: Lee Strobel
Subject: no clear claims

Ben, you've looked into this subject. Isn't it true that Jesus didn't come right out and say, "I'm God"? Doesn't that mean he didn't see himself as God? --Lee

RE: NO CLEAR CLAIMS

To: Lee Strobel
From: Ben Witherington
Subject: re: no clear claims

Lee—Don't forget when Jesus lived! If he'd simply announced, "Hi, folks; I'm God," that would have been heard as "I'm Yahweh," because the Jews of his day didn't have any concept of the Trinity—God as Father, Son, and Holy Spirit. They only knew of God the Father—whom they called Yahweh.

So if Jesus were to say he was God, that wouldn't have made any sense to them—and it would have hurt Jesus' efforts to get his message out. In private with his disciples—that was a different story, but the Gospels mainly tell us what Jesus did in public.

Make sense?—Ben

STATEMENT OF A SKEPTIC

The Jewish leaders may have been convinced about who Jesus claimed to be, but I was still skeptical. In fact, I was attracted to one of Jesus' own disciples, a guy named Thomas, because he was just as skeptical as I was. Even when all the other disciples were claiming that Jesus had returned to life (I decided to look into that claim, too; see chapter 9), Thomas said he wasn't going to believe a thing unless he could personally examine the wounds in Jesus' hands and feet.

According to the New Testament records, Jesus did appear and invite Thomas to check out the evidence for himself. Thomas the skeptic changed his tune and proclaimed, "My Lord and my God!" (See John 20:28.)

Jesus didn't respond by saying, "Wait a minute! Don't go calling me God—remember, I'm just a great teacher and a very moral man." Instead, Jesus said, "You believe because you see me. Those who believe without seeing me will be truly happy" (John 20:29, NCV).

Now, I'd like to be truly happy as much as the next guy, but I was by no means willing to buy into the notion that Jesus had actually died and returned to life. As far as I was concerned, his whole death could have been a hoax—how else could he show up after his supposed execution? What I was becoming convinced of, though, is that Jesus really did claim that he was God.

Which raises another question: Was Jesus lying?

WAS JESUS LYING WHEN HE CLAIMED TO BE GOD?

The fact that Jesus *claimed* to be God doesn't necessarily mean that he *was* God. After all, plenty of people pad the truth a little to make themselves seem more than they are—like the bench-warmer who says, "Sure, I'm a starter on the team," hoping to impress his date, or the girl who passes herself off as an experienced waitress on her first job application. A lot of people will lie when there's something in it for them.

So what was in it for Jesus?

DYING FOR A LIE?

Christ's oldest biography describes how he was asked point-blank during his trial: "Are you the Christ, the Son of

Jesus: Great Moral Teacher?

Some people suggest that Jesus was a great moral teacher, but he wasn't God.

That argument just won't work.

Great moral teachers don't lie and say that they are God. But Jesus did claim that he was God.

With Jesus, it seems to be all or nothing. Either he was a great moral teacher, in which case he wasn't lying when he said he was God, or he was lying, in which case he wasn't such a great moral teacher after all.

the Blessed One?" Jesus wasn't ambiguous. The first two words out of his mouth were: "I am."

The high priest knew what Jesus was saying, because he angrily told the court, "You have heard the blasphemy." What was blasphemous? That Jesus was claiming to be God! This, I learned, was the crime for which Jesus was put to death. (You can read about the trial in Mark 14:60–64. Granted, this information comes from the New Testament but, as you'll see in chapters 5 and 6, I found that there were good reasons for trusting the general reliability of the Bible's accounts of Jesus' life. You might want to withhold judgment until you get there.)

NO CLEAR CLAIMS

To: Ben Witherington
From: Lee Strobel
Subject: still not convinced

What makes you think Jesus was more than just a good teacher? I've heard that the idea that Jesus was more than that didn't get started until years after his death.

So what did Jesus get for claiming to be God? He got tortured to death.

Imagine somebody holding a gun to the bench-warmer's head and saying, "So what's the truth? Are you really a starting player? Because if you are, you're going to die." How long do you think the player's going to hold on to that lie?

Yet Jesus held to his claim right to the end. Would somebody willingly die for a claim he knew was a lie?

TAKING THE BULLET

There's a story about an Army sergeant and a private who were doing survival training in the Rocky Mountains. As they made their way through the woods, suddenly they encountered a big, angry grizzly bear that was about to attack them.

Quickly the sergeant sat down, ripped off his heavy hiking boots, grabbed a pair of running shoes out of his backpack, and pulled them on.

"What do you think you're doing?" yelled the private. "You'll never outrun that bear!"

"I don't have to," called the sergeant over his shoulder as he sprinted away. "I only have to outrun *you*."

You don't have to be a genius to know when a leader doesn't have your best interests at heart. Maybe you've played for a coach who was more concerned with his record than with what was best for the team. Or you've worked for a boss whose only goal was to make herself look good. In a situation where it's him or you, this kind of leader is going to save himself, as the sergeant was trying to do.

Who Jesus Thought He Was
- Jesus claimed to be God.
- That claim got him killed.

The question: Would Jesus be willing to die for a lie? Or was he willing to die because he believed he was telling the truth?

I know only one sure-fire way to determine whether a leader is really in my corner: *Is he willing to take a bullet that was meant for me?*

That's the kind of leader Jesus claimed to be. According to the gospel of Mark, Jesus told his followers that his purpose was "to give his life as a ransom for many." (See Mark 10:45.) He was willing to die a horrible death to pay for the sins of the world so that people could be made right with God. It would be like the sergeant in the story saying, "Private, you run for safety; I'll stay here and take on this bear."

It was becoming evident to me that Jesus didn't just claim to be God; he believed it. He wasn't pulling some kind of scam to get ahead by saying he was God. After all, what it got him was killed. And no one in his right mind dies for a lie.

Which raises another question: Was Jesus in his right mind?

Christianity: A Religion of Intolerance?

ne of Jesus' most outrageous claims is this: "I am the way and the truth and the life. No one comes to the Father except through me" (John 14:6).

Of all the incredible statements Jesus made, this is the one I found most offensive. If anyone else had said it, he'd be blasted as exclusive, intolerant, and narrow-minded. It's one thing to claim to be *a* way—but the *only* way to God? That sounds pretty judgmental.

The world is full of religions. The U.S. Constitution even defends your right to believe any religion you choose (or to believe none at all). Legally (at least in the United States), all religions are basically equal. A lot of people will tell you that there are a variety of paths people can take in their spiritual journey, and they all lead to the same God.

But as I looked into the claims of Christianity, I discovered one big difference between it and other religions. Other religions are based on people *doing* something to earn the favor of God. They must perform good deeds, chant the right words, use a Tibetan prayer wheel, go through a series of reincarnations, or faithfully follow other religious drills.

By contrast, Christianity is based on what, according to the Bible, Christ has already *done* on the cross. According to the Bible, nobody can do anything to *earn* God's favor; rather, Jesus offers forgiveness and eternal life as a gift.

Imagine two college frat houses. The first has a strict set of rules and allows in only people who have earned their membership. You have to accomplish something, get top grades, or measure up to a long list of requirements to qualify. No matter how hard they try, a lot of people just won't make the cut. They'll be excluded. That's what every other religion is like, because they're all based on the system of people doing something to earn God's approval.

But the other house throws its door wide open and says, "Anybody who wants membership is invited inside! Rich or poor, black or white, honor student or rebel, we would love to include you. All you need to get in is to accept this invitation." That, according to the Bible, is what Christianity is like.

Is Christ being offensive when he says that he is the *only* way to God? Judging by the number of people who are offended, you'd better believe it! Is Christ being exclusive? That's a different question. What do you think?

Was Jesus Crazy to Claim to Be God?

In one of the court cases I covered for the *Chicago Tribune,* a mild-mannered housewife stood accused of murdering her husband. At first glance she looked as wholesome as the mother on the Brady Bunch—well dressed, pleasant, kindly, looking as if she had just emerged from baking a fresh batch of chocolate-chip cookies for the neighborhood children. I rolled my eyes when a psychologist testified that she was mentally unable to stand trial.

Then her lawyer put her on the witness stand. At first her testimony was clear and rational. But it slowly became more and more bizarre as she described, calmly and with great seriousness, how she had been assaulted by one famous man after another, including the ghost of Napoleon. By the time she finished, nobody in the courtroom doubted that she was totally out of touch with reality. The judge committed her to a mental institution until she was well enough to face the charges against her.

How does all this relate to Jesus? In chapter 2 I retraced the evidence that showed Jesus meant it when he claimed to be God. That naturally raises the issue of whether Jesus was crazy when he made those claims.

DELUSIONS OF GRANDEUR?

There are a lot of nut cases running around who don't end up in mental institutions. Some of them even attract committed followers. Think about Marshall Herff Applewhite, for example—the leader of the Heaven's Gate cult who got all his disciples to put on new black Nikes, eat a tasty serving of poisoned pudding, then lie down and die in hopes that they'd be beamed up to the mother ship that would take them to some extra-terrestrial "Next Level."

Applewhite believed in his cause enough to die for it. So did Hitler. But they were both wrong. They both thought they were far greater, far more important than they really were. Maybe that's what happened with Jesus. (For other symptoms of mental imbalance, see the box, "Signs of Mental Instability.")

In an episode of *The Simpsons,* Homer gets sent to a mental hospital where his roommate claims to be Michael Jackson. The roommate does such a good impersonation that he convinces Bart over the phone that he really *is* Michael Jackson. Homer tells Bart that Michael will be coming home with him, and Bart brags to the whole neighborhood. When the car pulls up in front of the Simpson house, the mayor of Springfield, the local TV station, and all the neighborhood kids surge forward in anticipation. You can imagine the crowd's response when the celebrity they've been waiting for turns out to be a big, bald, white guy from New Jersey.

Signs of Mental Instability

Since it is obviously impossible to go back in time and get a psychological evaluation of Jesus, I interviewed a leading psychologist, Dr. Gary Collins, about insanity. He described some of the following symptoms psychologists look for to determine whether a person is mentally unbalanced.

Symptoms	Analyzing Jesus
INAPPROPRIATE EMOTIONS • **depression** for no known cause • out-of-proportion or irrational anger	JESUS' EMOTIONAL RESPONSES: • **Wept** at the death of his friend, Lazarus (see John 11:1–44). • Got angry **with** merchants taking advantage of the poor (see Luke 19:45–46). Would you say these are appropriate or inappropriate emotional responses?
MISPERCEPTIONS OR PARANOIA: **fearful** of imagined threats	• Accused one of his closest followers of plotting to betray him—but he turned out to be right (see Matthew 26:14–25, 47–50). • **Remained calm** and non-defensive at his trial (see Mark 15:1–15).
THINKING DISORDERS: can't carry on a **logical** conversation, **irrational**	According to Matthew 7:28–29, "the crowds were amazed at his teaching, because he taught as one who had authority." You can read one of Jesus' sermons in Matthew 5 and 6 and judge for yourself.

When a big, bald, white guy from New Jersey thinks he is *the* Michael Jackson, he's crazy. In fact, pretty much everybody who believes himself to be Michael Jackson is crazy—everybody but one. When Michael Jackson claims to be Michael Jackson, that's not crazy; that's the truth. (You may think that other things Michael Jackson does are a little crazy, but that's not the point here.) And if for some weird reason Michael Jackson decided to visit your neighborhood, people would know that's who it really was. For one thing, he'd look like Michael Jackson, not like some big, white, bald guy from New Jersey. He'd be able to moonwalk, and he'd know all the words to "Thriller." One way or another, there would be enough confirming evidence to convince the neighborhood celebrity-watchers that he was who he claimed to be.

It's only crazy to claim to be Michael Jackson if you aren't Michael Jackson.

It's only crazy to Claim to be God if you aren't God.

The question, then, is whether there is any confirming evidence that Jesus was who he said he was. It seems that some people had their doubts in Jesus' day. The gospel of John says that the things Jesus was saying "caused another split in the Jewish ranks. A lot of them were saying, 'He's crazy, a maniac—out of his head completely. Why bother listening to him?' But others weren't so sure: 'These aren't the words of a crazy man. Can a maniac open blind eyes?'" (John 10:19–21, *THE MESSAGE*)

At least some people, in Jesus' time as well as today, figured it wasn't crazy to claim to be God if you could back it up with the things Jesus was doing: "opening" eyes so blind people could see, healing the sick, walking on water, multiplying bread and fish so that a little bit could feed thousands of people—in short, miracles.

MIRACLE-WORKER OR MASTER HYPNOTIST?

If miracles were part of the evidence that Jesus was who he said he was, I wanted to know more about them. Now, I know that a lot of people, religious and non-religious alike, have no problem believing in miracles. (See box: "A Psychologist on the Supernatural.") But I was not one of those people. If something supernatural was supposed to happen, I would look at every possible natural cause—including the possibility of a hoax—before I would be willing to believe it was a miracle.

One of the most likely natural causes for Jesus' miracles I heard about was hypnotism.

A Psychologist on the Supernatural

"Our society today is caught up in 'spirituality.' That's a term that can mean almost anything, but it does recognize the supernatural. It's very interesting what psychologists believe in these days. Some are into Eastern mystical stuff; some talk about the power of shamans to influence people's lives.

"Twenty-five years ago, the suggestion of supernatural activity would have been immediately dismissed. Now many psychologists are beginning to recognize that maybe there are more things in heaven and earth than our philosophies can account for."

—Psychologist Gary Collins

Have you ever seen a hypnotist give water to someone in a trance and then suggest to him that he was drinking alcohol? The hypnotized person really believes it! He may even start to stagger just as if he'd put back a few too many Bud Lites before the show began.

Is it possible that this is how Jesus convinced the wedding guests at Cana that he had transformed jugs of water into fine wine? (You can read about that event in John 2:1–11.) If Jesus were a master hypnotist, could that explain the supposedly miraculous things he did?

As I looked into this possibility, I discovered certain facts about hypnosis as well as reports of miracles that challenged the hypnosis theory:

Hypnosis	Reported Miracles
INDIVIDUALS VS. LARGE GROUPS Hypnotists talk in a certain soothing tone of voice to the audience and watch for people who seem to be responding. Then they'll pick these people as volunteers, because they're readily susceptible to hypnosis. In a big group many people are resistant.	**WITNESSED BY LARGE GROUPS** Many of the miracles reported were witnessed by large groups, like the time Jesus fed 5000 men plus women and children (Matthew 14:13–21). Would all 5000-plus witnesses have been susceptible to hypnosis?
WILLING SUBJECTS You've probably heard that you can be hypnotized only if you want to be. To some extent, that's true. Generally, hypnosis doesn't work on people who are skeptics and doubters.	**UNWILLING SUBJECTS** Many of the miracles reported were witnessed by skeptics—like the Jewish leaders, who definitely did not want evidence that Jesus was God; or "doubting" Thomas; or Saul of Tarsus, who was so anti-Christ that he persecuted Christians until he underwent a miraculous conversion. (See Acts 9:1–19.)

As a hypothesis for explaining Jesus' miracles, I found the hypnosis theory less than satisfying. If the accounts in the New Testament could be trusted (I looked into that question, too; see chapters 5 and 6), it was beginning to look as if Jesus did back up his claims with some powerful evidence.

A MISSION THAT MATTERS

Have you ever looked at your life and thought, "Is this all there is?" Maybe things are even going pretty well for you, but somehow you're just not satisfied. You thought you'd be happier than you are. You expected that when you made the team or started this year in school or got certain grades or were going out with that particular person, you'd have it all together. But it's not enough. Something is missing.

One day when I was working at the *Chicago Tribune*, I went down the hall to the newspaper's library where clippings of articles are filed. I needed to look at a particular article I had written about a year earlier, so the librarian took me over to a huge file cabinet.

"We take one copy of every article," she said, "and we file it away under the name of the reporter who wrote it." She pulled out a broad, shallow file drawer, and inside were rows packed with yellow envelopes that were stamped LEE STROBEL. "Here you go," she said. "These are all your articles."

I had a strange sensation as I looked inside that drawer. Here was the substance of my entire life's work at the *Tribune*. Suddenly it struck me: *This is what I'm killing myself for?* I'm trading my life for a drawer full of neatly folded newspaper clippings that are turning brittle and yellowing around the edges? At that moment, it didn't seem like a fair trade. I was getting ripped off!

Some people trade their entire life for a drawer full of shopping receipts, or for a shelf full of trophies, or for notches on their bedpost, or for a collection of empty bottles. Is it really a fair trade?

That's what struck me as I looked at Jesus' life. He gave his life for a mission he believed in so deeply that he was willing to die for it—no regrets. I had to ask myself, what's crazier: Living and even dying for a cause you really believe in, or just running with the rat race until you die?

What's crazier :
Living and even dying for a cause
you really believe in,
or just running with the rat race
until you die?

As far as I could tell, Jesus didn't show any of the signs of mental illness or insanity. I couldn't blow off his claims to be God simply by saying he was crazy. But Jesus' claims about himself weren't just a generic statement like, "I'm God." Jesus claimed to have a very specific identity: he claimed to be the Messiah. The Old Testament is full of descriptions of what the one and only Messiah would be. Did Jesus measure up?

Did Jesus Match the Identity of the Messiah?

i've written a lot of articles over the years on predictions about the future—it's one of those New Year's stories that all beginning reporters get stuck doing—and I know how few predictions actually come true. For instance, every year people in Chicago insist that the Cubs are going to clinch the World Series, and *that* certainly hasn't come true in my lifetime!

In the Jewish Scriptures, which Christians call the Old Testament, there are several dozen major prophecies about the coming of the Messiah, who would be sent by God to redeem his people. These predictions provide a way for the Israelites to rule out any impostors and check the credentials of the authentic Messiah.

The Greek word for "Messiah" is *Christ*. But was Jesus really the Christ? Did he fulfill these predictions that were written hundreds of years before he was born?

A NICE JEWISH BOY FROM NEW JERSEY

For an insider's look at the Old Testament prophecies, I decided to talk with Louis Lapides. He grew up in a Jewish family in Newark, New Jersey. For someone with his heritage, the question of whether Jesus is the long-anticipated Messiah goes beyond theory. It's intensely personal. I wanted to hear about his investigation of this issue.

LOOKING FOR A RELIGION THAT WORKS

"My parents got divorced when I was seventeen," Lapides told me—and even after all these years I could still hear the hurt in his voice. "That's when I gave up whatever faith I had. I wondered, *Where does God come in? Why didn't they go to a rabbi for counseling? What good is religion if it can't help people in a practical way?* It sure couldn't keep my parents together. When they split up, part of me split as well.

Does God **relate** to my **struggles?**
Does he care about **me** as an **individual?**

"On top of that, in Judaism I didn't feel as if I had a personal relationship with God. I had a lot of beautiful ceremonies and traditions, but our God was a distant God who said, 'Here are the rules—you live by them, you'll be OK; I'll see you later.' And there I was, an adolescent with raging hormones, wondering, *Does God relate to my problems? Does he care about me as an individual?* Well, not in any way I could see."

Not long after his parents' divorce, Lapides was drafted. By 1967 he found himself on the other side of the world in a cargo boat whose freight—ammunition, bombs, rockets, and other high explosives—made it a tempting target for the Vietcong.

Lapides recalled, "In our orientation in Vietnam, they told us, 'Twenty percent of you will probably get killed, and the other 80 percent of you will probably get a sexually transmitted disease or become alcoholics or get hooked on drugs.' I thought, *I don't even have a 1 percent chance of coming out normal!*"

He survived Vietnam, returning home with a taste for marijuana and an interest in Eastern religions. "I went to Buddhist meetings, but that was empty," he said. "I went to Scientology meetings, but they were too manipulative and controlling. Hinduism believed in gods who would have all these crazy orgies, and in gods who were blue elephants. None of it made sense; none of it was satisfying."

"I CAN'T BELIEVE IN JESUS"

One religion Lapides refused to consider was Christianity. Whenever anyone would bring up the name of Jesus, Lapides would fend him off with his stock answer. "I'm Jewish," he would say. "I can't believe in Jesus."

Then one day a pastor challenged him. "Do you know of the prophecies about the Messiah?" he asked.

Lapides was taken off guard. "Prophecies?" he said. "I've never heard of them."

The minister startled Lapides by referring to some of the Old Testament predictions. *Wait a minute!* Lapides thought. *Those are my Jewish Scriptures he's quoting! How could Jesus be in there?*

When the pastor offered him a Bible, Lapides was skeptical. "Is the New Testament in there?" he asked. The pastor nodded. "OK, I'll read the Old Testament, but I'm not going to open up the other one," Lapides told him.

He was surprised by the minister's response. "Fine," said the pastor. "Just read the Old Testament and ask the God of Abraham, Isaac, and Jacob—the God of Israel—to show you if Jesus is the Messiah. Because he *is* your Messiah. He came to the Jewish people first, and then he also became the Savior of the world."

To Lapides, this was new information. Intriguing information. Astonishing information. So he went back to his apartment, opened the Old Testament to its first book, Genesis, and went hunting for Jesus among words that had been written hundreds of years before the carpenter of Nazareth had been born.

A PORTRAIT OF JESUS

"Pretty soon," Lapides told me, "I was reading the Old Testament every day and finding one prophecy after another."

As Lapides worked through the Scriptures, he was stopped cold by Isaiah 53 (see box: Predictions of the Messiah). Here was the picture of a Messiah who would suffer and die for the sins of Israel and the world—all written more than 700 years before Jesus walked the earth.

Instantly Lapides recognized the portrait: this was Jesus of Nazareth! Jews in the Old Testament tried to pay for their sins through a system of animal sacrifices; here was Jesus, the ultimate sacrifice, who paid for sin once and for all. Here was the personification of God's plan of redemption.

This discovery was so amazing that Lapides could come to only one conclusion: it was a fraud! He believed that Christians had rewritten the Old Testament and twisted Isaiah's words to make it sound as if the prophet had been foreshadowing Jesus.

And if this was just a hoax, then Lapides wanted to expose it. "I asked my stepmother to send me a Jewish Bible so I could check it out myself," he told me. "She did, and guess what? It said the same thing! Now I really had to deal with it."

BECOMING WHOLE

Lapides and some friends headed into the Mojave Desert for a getaway. Spiritually he was feeling conflicted. He had

Predictions of the Messiah

He was despised and rejected by men,
  a man of sorrows, and familiar with suffering.
Like one from whom men hide their faces
  he was despised, and we esteemed him not.
Surely he took up our infirmities
  and carried our sorrows,
yet we considered him stricken by God,
  smitten by him, and afflicted.
But he was pierced for our transgressions,
  he was crushed for our iniquities;
the punishment that brought us peace
    was upon him,
  and by his wounds we are healed.
We all, like sheep, have gone astray,
  each of us has turned to his own way;
and the Lord has laid on him
  the iniquity of us all.
He was oppressed and afflicted,
  yet he did not open his mouth;
he was led like a lamb to the slaughter,
  and as a sheep before her shearers is silent,
  so he did not open his mouth.
By oppression and judgment he was taken away.
  And who can speak of his descendants?
For he was cut off from the land of the living;
  for the transgression of my people he was stricken.
He was assigned a grave with the wicked,
  and with the rich in his death,
though he had done no violence,
  nor was any deceit in his mouth....
For he bore the sin of many,
  and made intercession for the transgressors.

Isaiah 53:3–9, 12

Did Jesus Match the Identity of the Messiah?

nightmares of being torn apart by dogs pulling at him from opposite directions. Sitting among the desert scrub, he remembered what someone had once told him: "You're either on God's side or on Satan's side."

After all he had seen in Vietnam, he knew about evil—and that's not the side he wanted to be on. So Lapides prayed, "God, I've got to come to the end of this struggle. I have to know beyond the shadow of doubt that Jesus is the Messiah. I need to know that you, as the God of Israel, want me to believe this."

As he told me the story, Lapides hesitated, unsure how to put into words what happened next. "The best way I can describe what happened is that God spoke to my heart. He convinced me that he exists. And out in the desert, in my heart I said, 'God, I accept Jesus into my life. I don't understand what I'm supposed to do with him, but I want him. I've pretty much made a mess of my life; I need you to change me.'"

And, Lapides said, God began to do that in a process that continues to this day. "My friends knew my life had changed, and they couldn't understand it," he said. "They'd say, 'Something happened to you in the desert. You don't want to do drugs anymore. There's something different about you.'

"My friends **knew** my life had changed, and they couldn't **understand** it."

"I would say, 'Well, I can't explain it either. All I know is that there's someone in my life, and it's someone who's holy, who's righteous—and I just feel whole.'"

That last word, it seemed, said everything. *"Whole,"* he emphasized to me, "in a way I had never felt before."

PROBING THE PROPHECIES

When I read Isaiah 53 in the Old Testament, like Lapides I found it to be an uncanny description of Jesus' being crucified—and yet it was written more than 700 years before the fact. That's like my trying to predict how the Cubs will do in the year 2700! In all, there are about five dozen major prophecies concerning the Messiah, and the more I studied them, the more difficulty I had trying to explain them away.

MESSIANIC MANEUVERING?

My first line of defense was that Jesus may have intentionally maneuvered his life to fulfill the prophecies so that he would be mistaken for the Messiah. For instance, Zechariah 9:9 predicted that the Messiah would ride a donkey into Jerusalem. Maybe when Jesus was getting ready to enter the town, he told his disciples, "Go fetch me a donkey. I want to fool these people into thinking I'm the Messiah. After all, I'm anxious to get tortured to death!"

But that argument fell apart when I read prophecies about events that Jesus never could have arranged, such as the place of his birth (which the prophet Micah had predicted hundreds of years in advance), his family tree, how he was betrayed for a specific amount of money, how he was put to death, how his bones remained unbroken (unlike the two criminals who were crucified with him), how the soldiers cast lots for his clothing, and on and on (see box).

COINCIDENCE?

My second line of defense was that Jesus might have fulfilled these prophecies by coincidence. Maybe several people in history have fit these predictions, but Jesus happened to have a better public relations agent and so now he's the one everyone remembers.

But reading a book by Dr. Peter Stoner, a science professor, undermined that objection. Stoner worked with 600 students to come up with their best estimate of the mathematical

Could Jesus have arranged his life to fulfill these prophecies?

	PROPHECIES	JESUS' LIFE
PLACE OF BIRTH	"But you, Bethlehem Ephrathah, though you are small among the clans of Judah, out of you will come for me one who will be ruler over Israel, whose origins are from of old, from ancient times." (Micah 5:2)	Jesus was born in Bethlehem. (See Matthew 2:1)
FAMILY TREE	"'A new day is coming,' announces the Lord. 'At that time I will raise up from David's royal line a true and rightful branch.... And the Branch will be called The Lord Who Makes Us Right With Himself.'" (Jeremiah 23:5, 6, NIrV)	Jesus was a descendent of David.
BLOOD MONEY	"I told them, 'If you think it best, give me my pay, but if not, keep it,' So they paid me thirty pieces of silver. And the Lord said to me, 'Throw it to the potter'—the handsome price at which they priced me!' So I took the thirty pieces of silver and threw them into the house of the Lord to the potter." (Zechariah 11:12–13)	Judas Iscariot betrayed Jesus for thirty silver coins. Later Judas threw the money into the temple and left, and the priests decided to use the money to buy a potter's field. (Matthew 26:15; 27:5, 7)
GAMBLING OVER CLOTHES	"They divide my garments among them and cast lots for my clothing." (Psalm 22:18)	While Jesus was being crucified, soldiers gambled for his clothes by casting lots. (See Matthew 27:35)

The Case for Christ

probability of just 8 Old Testament prophecies being fulfilled in any one person living down to the present time. Stoner then calculated that the probability of anyone fulfilling all 8 would be one chance in a hundred million billion. That's a figure with 17 zeroes behind it!

Want a more human, less mathematical, picture of those odds? Imagine the entire world covered with white tile that is one-and-a-half inches square—every bit of dry land on the planet—with a gold star painted on the bottom of just one of the tiles.

Then picture a person being allowed to wander for a lifetime around all 7 continents. He would be permitted to bend down only one time and pick up a single piece of tile. What are the odds it would be the one tile with the gold star on its reverse side? One chance in a hundred million billion—the same as just 8 of the Old Testament prophecies coming true in any one person throughout history!

Now, you can agree or disagree with the estimates that the students came up with for Stoner's calculations. After all, prophecies can be difficult to quantify and assessments can vary. You could come up with your own estimates and do your own calculations. But when I examined the prophecies myself, I had to agree with Stoner's conclusion: the chances of anyone coincidentally fulfilling these ancient predictions would surely be prohibitive.

A WORTHWHILE INVESTMENT?

Jesus said he came to fulfill the prophecies. He said, "Everything must be fulfilled that is written about me in the Law of Moses, the Prophets and the Psalms" (Luke 24:44). I was beginning to believe that they really were fulfilled—only in Jesus Christ.

I imagined being offered a business deal with just one chance in a hundred million billion that I'd lose. I'd put everything I owned into a sure-fire winner like that! And I was starting to think, "With odds like that, maybe I should think about investing my life in Christ."

But just as I wouldn't invest in a stock without making sure the source of information was reliable, I wouldn't invest my life in Jesus without checking out the reliability of the information on him—the New Testament.

Living and Forgiving Like God

DOES JESUS MATCH THE DESCRIPTION OF GOD?

The Old Testament gives details about the God of the Bible that sketch out very specifically what he's like. Now, Jesus claims to be God. But does he match the sketch of God that we find elsewhere in the Bible? If he doesn't, we can conclude that his claim to being God is false. Two important qualities of God have to do with sin: God himself is sinless, and God can forgive sins. How does Jesus match up?

God

Jesus

CAN FORGIVE SINS

According to the Bible, God is the one in charge of forgiving sin. When King David committed adultery and then arranged the death of the woman's husband, he said to God, "Against you, you only, have I sinned" (Psalm 51:4). David recognized that, although he had hurt people, in the end he had sinned against God, and he needed God to forgive him.

OFFERED FORGIVENESS FOR SINS

One of the most striking—and offensive, to many people—things that Jesus did was to forgive sin. (You can read one account in Mark 2:1-12.) Think about it: If you do something against me, I have the right to forgive you. But if you do something against me and somebody else comes along and says, "I forgive you," what kind of arrogance is that? The only person who would have that right would be God.

IS MORALLY PERFECT AND HOLY

The Old Testament prophet Isaiah made the contrast between people (sinful) and God (sinless) pretty clear. (See Isaiah 5:15-16 for an example.) Right after that, things got personal for Isaiah when he encountered God in a vision. While heavenly creatures were shouting, "Holy, holy, holy!" about God, Isaiah was crying, "I'm doomed! Everything I say is sinful, and so are the words of everyone around me" (Isaiah 6:3, 5, CEV).

CLAIMED TO BE MORALLY PERFECT AND HOLY

Not only did Jesus forgive sin, he claimed to be sinless himself. Jesus said, with a straight face, "Can any of you prove me guilty of sin?" (John 8:46.) If I said that, my friends and family and everybody who knows me would be glad to stand up and testify. But it seems that the better people got to know Jesus, the more they marveled at his integrity. Two of his closest companions, John and Peter, wrote, "In him is no sin" (1 John 3:5), and "He didn't commit any sin. No lies ever came out of his mouth" (1 Peter 2:22, NIrV).

The Case for Christ

HOW RELIABLE IS THE INFORMATION ABOUT CHRIST?

two

Can You Trust Christ's Biographies?

heck out the biography section at your local Barnes & Noble and you'll find shelves of books, from scholarly works to "unauthorized" tell-all stories, about famous and not-so-famous people. Depending on which sources you read, you could come away with very different pictures of the same person. Take Elvis, for example: According to most sources, he died on August 16, 1977, and is buried in Memphis, Tennessee. But if you consult the *National Enquirer,* you'll read that Elvis was recently seen alive and presumably well in Kalamazoo, Michigan. It only makes sense to figure that one of these reports isn't completely accurate.

Jesus' oldest biographies are the books in the New Testament of the Bible called the Gospels and named after their writers: Matthew, Mark, Luke, and John. From these biographies, I found out a lot about who Jesus claimed to be (see chapter 2), what kind of evidence there was for his sanity (chapter 3), and how he fit the bill of the predicted Messiah (chapter 4). For the time being, I set aside the issue of whether the Bible really was the inspired word of God. Instead, I took the Bible for what it undeniably is—a collection of ancient documents claiming to record historical events.

The question is, is that collection of ancient documents reliable in what it reports?

HOW MANY EYEBALLS?

I began my investigation by asking the first question any good journalist asks: "How many eyeballs are there?" The term "eyeball" is slang for eyewitness. After years of reporting on courtroom trials, I know how convincing eyewitness testimony can be in establishing whether an event happened the way people claim it did. Believe me, I've seen plenty of defendants sent to prison by eyewitnesses.

Consistency and Contradictions

One of the arguments I'd often heard against believing what the Gospels say is that they contradict one another. How can two Gospels both be accurate if they give different accounts of the same event?

A surprising discovery is that many historians consider minor variations to be evidence in favor of the truth of an account. The idea is that if the writers were lying, they'd make sure to get their stories straight—and they'd agree in every detail. What seems to be a contradiction is often just the same event viewed from a different perspective.

For details on some specific areas of apparent contradiction, see the box "Contradictory Evidence?"

So I wanted to know, "How many witnesses met this person named Jesus? How many heard his teachings? How many watched him perform miracles? How many actually saw him after he supposedly returned from the dead?" Are these accounts backed up by credible witnesses, or are they tabloid thrillers invented by some weirdo in the first-century equivalent of Kalamazoo?

It turns out that there wasn't just a single eyewitness; there were many. The historian Mark recorded Peter's firsthand account in what is now called the gospel of Mark. Luke, a physician and a sort of first-century investigative reporter, wrote a biography of Jesus based on eyewitness testimony, too. But we don't have to settle for "what he said that she said"— the New Testament doesn't just give secondhand reports about this eyewitness testimony; it contains actual writings by several of the eyewitnesses themselves. For instance, Peter himself wrote two letters that are included in what is now the New Testament. Matthew, John, and James were all eyewitnesses who wrote biographies or letters about Jesus.

Peter insisted that he was accurately recording firsthand information. "We did not follow cleverly invented stories when we told you about the power and coming of our Lord Jesus Christ," he wrote, "but we were eyewitnesses of his majesty" (2 Peter 1:16).

John said he was writing about things "which we have heard, which we have seen with our eyes, which we have looked at and our hands have touched" (1 John 1:1).

The New Testament biographies of Jesus aren't just secondhand information. They are based on eyewitness accounts.

AN INFORMED AUDIENCE

Of course, eyewitnesses can lie. I could tell you all about the homecoming game my senior year in high school. I could give you a play-by-play of our struggle against the top-ranked

You Lie, You Die

As a journalist, I've come across a fair number of liars. In my experience, people usually lie because they figure it will get them something they want—or get them out of something they definitely don't want.

I might be tempted to lie to you about making a winning touchdown if I think it will get me respect. (Of course, this backfires as soon as you discover that I wasn't even on the football team.) You might lie about cheating on an exam if you think it will get you out of a detention or a failing grade. But what was in it for the disciples if they were lying about Jesus? Their claims that he was God got them criticism, persecution, and ultimately death.

What do you think? Would all those eyewitnesses risk their lives for a lie?

team in the state, concluding with a dramatic finish in which I (I will modestly admit) made the winning touchdown only seconds before the end of the fourth quarter. While you might suspect me of exaggerating, you couldn't know for sure whether I was reporting it accurately or not. After all, you weren't there. On the other hand, if I tried to tell you about *your* homecoming game, and you had been right in the stands or on the playing field yourself, you'd have a lot better chance of spotting any inaccuracies or outright lies in my version.

The eyewitnesses who wrote about Jesus were preaching to people who lived at the same time and in the same area that Jesus did. This is important, because if the disciples were exaggerating or rewriting history, their audiences would have known it and called them on it—in the same way that you would catch me in a lie about your homecoming game.

The Case for Christ

I had to ask myself, "Would **Christianity** have taken root as quickly as it did if these **disciples** were saying *things* that their **audiences** knew were exaggerated or false?"

Shortly after Jesus was killed, Peter spoke to a crowd in the same city where the crucifixion had taken place. Many of the people listening had probably seen Jesus put to death. Peter started out by saying: "Men of Israel, listen to this: Jesus of Nazareth was a man accredited by God to you by miracles, wonders and signs, which God did among you through him, *as you yourselves know*" (Acts 2:22).

In other words, "C'mon, everybody—you know what Jesus did. You saw these things for yourself!" Then he went on to say, "God has raised this Jesus to life, and we are all witnesses of the fact" (Acts 2:32).

The audience's reaction was very interesting. They didn't say, "We don't know what you're talking about!" or, "That's not the way it really happened!" Instead, they panicked and wanted to know what they should do. On that day about 3,000 people asked for forgiveness and many others followed— apparently because they knew that Peter was telling the truth. (You can read the whole story for yourself in Acts 2:14–47.)

I had to ask myself, "Would Christianity have taken root as quickly as it did if these disciples were saying things that their audiences knew were exaggerated or false?"

20/30 HINDSIGHT?

As I was becoming more confident in the New Testament's eyewitness accounts, one issue kept coming back to me. The eyewitnesses didn't write down their accounts as the events happened. They were passed along verbally for a period of time. Some estimates suggest that the Gospels weren't written until a hundred or more years after Jesus died. I'd heard claims that myths about Jesus had grown up between his death and

Contradictory Evidence?

The four biographies of Jesus—Matthew, Mark, Luke, and John—don't always tell the same story in exactly the same way. Supporters of Jesus say that the accounts don't contradict each other, but rather describe the same events from different perspectives.

Here are two examples and the possible explanations I uncovered. You can decide for yourself whether the explanations seem reasonable.

STORY	CONTRADICTION?	POSSIBLE EXPLANATION
Jesus heals a Roman commander's servant (described in Matthew 8:5-13 and Luke 7:1-10).	• Matthew says that the commander asked Jesus to heal his servant. • Luke says that the commander sent others to ask Jesus to heal the servant.	Just as we might say, "The President announced a new foreign policy today," when actually the announcement was written by a speechwriter and delivered by the press secretary, so in New Testament times people would say that an official (like the commander) did something, even if he did it through others.
Jesus' genealogies (found in Matthew 1:1-16 and Luke 3:23-38)	Different people are listed in the two genealogies.	• Matthew may give Joseph's (Jesus' father) side of the family tree; Luke may give Mary's side of the family tree. • Another possible explanation is that both genealogies are of Joseph's side, but Luke gives the biological line and Matthew gives the legal line—which is different because of Old Testament laws about inheritance.

If you're interested in studying some of the other apparent contradictions in the New Testament for yourself, two good books to look at are *The Encyclopedia of Biblical Difficulties* by Gleason L. Archer and *When Critics Ask* by Norman Geisler and Thomas Howe.

the time the New Testament was written—myths that distorted the truth beyond recognition.

But as I checked out the facts, I found out that recent archaeological discoveries have forced scholars to give earlier and earlier estimates about when the New Testament was written. I'm not an expert in archaeology myself (I didn't score that winning touchdown, either), so I investigated some of the conclusions of people who are.

Dr. William Albright, who used to direct the American School of Oriental research in Jerusalem and later taught at Johns Hopkins University, says he's convinced that the different books of the New Testament were written within 50 years (not 100) after Jesus died—and more likely closer to 45 years. Another scholar, Craig Blomberg, thinks the time gap was about 30 years between Jesus' death and when Mark wrote his gospel. This means that the New Testament was available in written form while plenty of eyewitnesses were still alive to say either, "Yes, that's the way it happened," or, "I was there, and that's not what I saw!"

One of the biggest questions about Christianity is whether Jesus' resurrection is real or a myth. (You can read more about that question in chapters 7, 8, and 9.) Whatever decision you come to on that question, you can't take the easy way out by saying that it's a myth that grew up decades or even a century after Jesus' death. This timeline shows why.

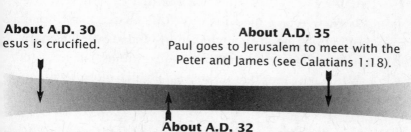

About A.D. 30
Jesus is crucified.

About A.D. 35
Paul goes to Jerusalem to meet with the Peter and James (see Galatians 1:18).

About A.D. 32
The apostle Paul is converted on the road to Damascus. (You can read about it in Acts 9.) He goes to Damascus to meet with Christians and receive instruction.

Can You Trust Christ's Biographies?

Sometime during those visits with Christian leaders and his early training in the Christian faith, Paul was taught a creed—a statement of belief—that the Christian church was already using to declare its belief in Christ's resurrection. How do we know? Because Paul described it:

> What I received I passed on to you. And it is the most important of all. Here is what it is. Christ died for our sins, just as Scripture said he would. He was buried. He was raised from the dead on the third day, just as Scripture said he would be. He appeared to Peter.
>
> Then he appeared to the Twelve. After that, he appeared to more than 500 believers at the same time. Most of them are still living. But some have died. He appeared to James, Then he appeared to all the apostles. Last of all, he also appeared to me.
>
> (1 Corinthians 15:3–8, NIrV)

Do you see what that means? By the time Paul got his lessons in Christianity 101 in Damascus and Jerusalem, the Christian church was already teaching that Christ died for sins, was buried, and was raised from the dead. That's the creed Paul "received" and "passed on." This wasn't 100 years or 50 years or even 30 years after Jesus' death; this was 2 to 5 years after Jesus' death. And experts said that's far too fast for legend to have developed and wiped out a core of historical truth.

I couldn't deny the importance of that evidence. It certainly seemed to take the wind out of the charge that Christ's resurrection was merely a myth that developed over long periods of time as legends corrupted the eyewitness accounts of Christ's life. For me, this struck especially close to home, because it was one of my biggest objections to Christianity.

PLAYING TELEPHONE

I had another objection ready, though. When I hold a Bible in my hand, what I'm really holding are *copies* of the ancient

The Case for Christ

historical records. The original manuscripts of the biographies of Jesus—Matthew, Mark, Luke, and John—and all the other books of the Old and New Testaments have long ago crumbled into dust. And when I say "copies," I don't mean photocopies, obviously. These copies were made by hand by a lot of people over a lot of years.

I pictured it sort of like that game little kids play called "telephone." One kid whispers something into another kid's ear—like, "All cows eat grass"—and the second kid whispers it to the third kid who whispers it to the fourth kid and so on, mumbling and giggling the way people do when they're whispering, until what the kid at the end of the line hears is, "I have lousy gas."

Actually, though, that's not an accurate picture of how the Bible got copied. A better analogy would be something like this: The kid starting the telephone game whispers something to two different kids. Each of those kids whispers to two more kids. They whisper to two more kids. And so it goes, until at the end of the line you have not one version, but dozens and dozens of versions of the original statement. If one final version is, "Jesus is bored," another is, "Pieces of board," and a third is, "Freeze us a gourd," you've got a pretty good idea that the original message got distorted along the way. But what if all the final versions are the same? What if almost every kid at the end of every line ends up with, "Jesus is Lord"?

There are over 5,000 copies of New Testament manuscripts copied in Greek. And 8,000 to 10,000 in Latin. Eight thousand more in other languages such as Ethiopic, Slavic, and Armenian. Throw in a few miscellaneous other manuscripts, and there are 24,000 New Testament manuscripts in all. (For a comparison with other old writings, see the box "Ancient Manuscripts.")

The amazing thing is that they say the same thing! You'll find some variations in spelling and stuff like that, but 99.5

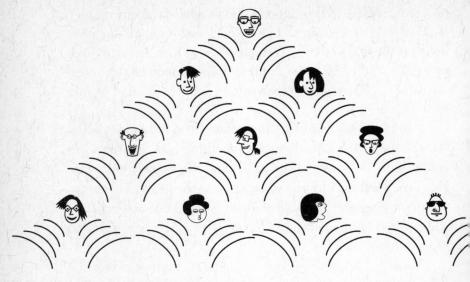

percent of the manuscripts match up. Undoubtedly the people copying the New Testament made some mistakes as they wrote. But, unlike the telephone game, where half the fun is in making mistakes, these guys were serious about their work. After all, they considered these documents to be sacred. The variations between the manuscripts, in the end, have turned out to be as minor as a few typos in a few insignificant words in an entire Sunday newspaper.

If I heard 29 kids at the end of 30 telephone games all saying, "Jesus is Lord," I'd figure that's what the original statement was. When 24,000 New Testament manuscripts say virtually the same thing, it makes sense that they are accurate copies of the original.

WORDS THAT WORK

Right now you may be thinking, "Fine. The New Testament was written by eyewitnesses who really saw Jesus. It was first heard and read by people who could have debunked it if it were a bunch of lies. The Bibles we have today are accurate

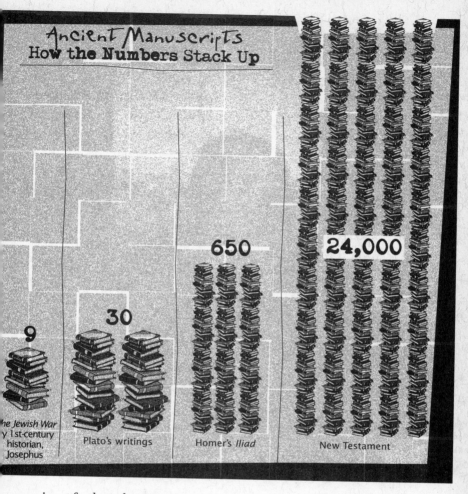

Ancient Manuscripts
How the Numbers Stack Up

9

The Jewish War
by 1st-century
historian,
Josephus

30

Plato's writings

650

Homer's *Iliad*

24,000

New Testament

copies of what the eyewitnesses originally wrote. Big deal. We've got a really old, really accurate book. What does it have to do with me?"

Here's what happened to me when I got serious enough to pursue that question. Most of the important relationships in my life were a little rocky. When I looked at them honestly, there was room for improvement. I started listening to Christian messages on relationships, and as I did, I had to admit that the principles in the Bible made sense. Of course, Christians believed that these ideas made sense because they were from God. I wasn't ready to buy that premise, but I was willing to try the principles simply because they sounded so reasonable. When I began treating my friends and my family the way the Bible said to, guess what happened? My relationships improved!

As I started applying the Bible's wisdom to the way I dealt with my anger, I found my emotions coming under control. When I started practicing forgiveness the way the Bible prescribes, it eased the bitterness that used to make my stomach churn and my jaw clench. And this happened again and again, in the area of finances, stress, character qualities—you name it.

After a while I said to myself, "Maybe there *is* something to the Bible. When I try living the way it says I should live, my life gets better. Where did all that wisdom come from? Is it possible that the Bible really is a revelation from God?"

My ultimate conclusion was: Yes. I was convinced that the Bible is God's inspired Word—not just because I checked out its historical reliability, but also because I personally experienced the way it could make my life better, even though I wasn't yet a Christian.

Maybe you've come to the same conclusion. Or maybe not. Maybe you'd like a little more evidence that the Bible is what it claims to be. If so, the next chapter is for you.

Is There a Case for Christ Outside the Bible?

t's 11:35 P.M. when you pull the car into the driveway. As you open the car door, a blinding light shines full in your face, and a voice says, "Hold it right there! We've got some questions to ask you."

After a brief recitation of your rights, a uniformed officer informs you that a driver your age in a vehicle of the same make as yours is wanted for questioning in connection with a series of crimes committed over the past four hours. You are invited to share anything that might persuade the officer that you are not that driver.

Quickly you explain that you spent the evening in a law-abiding fashion. You picked up some friends and went to McDonald's, where you noticed that the Happy Meal toy was a promotion for the latest animated film—not that you ordered a Happy Meal; you had value meal #3, super-sized, and you had to finish the fries in the car in order to make it to the 8:15 showing of the new James Bond movie. One of your friends must have stepped in some gum on the theater floor, because when you got back in the car he noticed that it was all over the floor mat, so you spent a little time in the parking lot scraping the floor mat with the leftover napkins from McDonald's before going to Baker's Square for a piece of pie—cherry-rhubarb—then dropping your friends off and coming straight home.

As you finish your story, the officer who was scribbling notes says to her partner, "I'll call the theater and see what time the James Bond movie was showing tonight." The other officer flashes a warrant and tells you that he's going to look—very closely—inside your car.

Now suppose the floor mats show no more than the usual amount of grime, and the officer finds no evidence of half-eaten french fries wedged between the seats. Does that mean that your story is all lies and you're headed for a certain conviction? Of course not. (Although it probably won't help your case any.)

On the other hand, suppose "routine investigation" reveals that the McDonald's you mentioned is in fact giving away the toy you described in its Happy Meals; the theater did show the Bond film at 8:15; Baker's Square is currently serving cherry-rhubarb pie; and to top it off you have an almost-empty, super-sized carton of McDonald's fries in your car and a scrap of napkin stuck to some gum on the passenger's floor mat. Are you home free? Not necessarily, but your credibility is certainly higher.

CORROBORATING EVIDENCE

What about the credibility of the Bible? We've talked about the evidence *within* the Bible for the case for Christ (see chapter 5). But what about evidence *outside* the Bible? If Christ is for real, and the Bible is true, I shouldn't have to take just the Bible's word on it; I ought to be able to find some corroborating evidence for the claim that Jesus is God.

What I found is a lot like the french-fry carton in your back seat. It doesn't settle anything one way or another. If you take it as absolute proof of the validity of the Bible and of Christ's claims, then you're doing a sloppy job of investigating. On the other hand, if you write it off as irrelevant, then you're being more closed-minded than you'd probably like to admit.

My challenge to myself was to check out the evidence in a fair-minded way. My challenge to you is the same.

BEYOND THE BIBLICAL BIOGRAPHIES

Did Jesus really live, or is he a fictional character found only in the Bible?

If you never read the Bible or any Christian writings, you could learn the following about Jesus from an ancient Jewish work called the Talmud and from ancient historical writers such as Josephus, Tacitus, and Pliny the Younger. (You've got to wonder what *his* parents were thinking when they named him.)

Jesus was a Jewish teacher.

Many people believed he performed healings and other miracles.

Some people believed he was the long-awaited Messiah.

He was rejected by the Jewish leaders.

He was crucified under the authority of Pontius Pilate in the reign of Tiberius.

Despite this shameful death, his followers, who believed that he was still alive, spread beyond Palestine so that there were large numbers of them in Rome by A.D. 64.

All kinds of people from the cities and the countryside—men and women, slave and free—worshiped him as God.

DIGGING FOR DETAILS

Maybe you find the thought of a police officer digging through the trash in your car to find french-fry cartons and pre-chewed bubble gum a little disgusting. But in essence, that's what archaeologists do, only with older piles of junk.

Archaeology can do three things with respect to the Bible:

It can uncover evidence that contradicts the Bible. For example, John 5:2 describes the pool of Bethesda as having five covered porches. Suppose that archaeological digs uncover a pool at that site that clearly has only three porches. That evidence would contradict what the Bible says and cast doubt on the accuracy of the New Testament. (Actually, however, an excavation uncovered a pool with five covered porches at that site.) Scholars have concluded that no archaeological evidence found to date flat-out contradicts the Bible.

Archaeology can uncover no evidence relating to the Bible one way or the other. Remember Indiana Jones in "Raiders of the Lost Ark"? Like him, lots of people have looked for the remains of the ark of the covenant described in the Old Testament. Unlike the movie version, however, no one has yet found it. Does that mean that the ark never existed? Not any more than the absence of McDonald's trash in your car means you never ate at McDonald's. You really can't draw a scientifically valid conclusion one way or the other from the *absence* of archaeological evidence.

Archaeology can uncover evidence that confirms what the Bible says. Since I didn't find any evidence in the first category (contradicting the Bible), and you can't base a lot of conclusions on the second category, this third category is the one I spent some time checking out.

Archaeology, like most sciences, involves drawing conclusions from the evidence. You know as well as I do that two different people can draw two different conclusions from the same evidence. (Think, for example, about the lowest grade on your last report card. Your conclusion might be that you are not gifted in that subject and so you should focus your energies elsewhere. Your parent's conclusion, on the other hand, might be that you should spend more—much more—time on that subject.)

If archaeology shows that the New Testament writers were accurate in reporting historical and geographical details, does this increase your confidence that they would be similarly careful in recording events about Jesus? Why or why not?

I wouldn't have been surprised to discover that archaeologists who were Christians interpreted the evidence as confirming biblical accounts, while archaeologists who were atheists or agnostics would be more skeptical. That's why I was especially fascinated by the story of Sir William Ramsay of Oxford University in England, one of history's greatest archaeologists. He was an atheist. He spent 25 years doing archaeological digs to try to disprove the book of Acts, which was written by the historian Luke (who also wrote the gospel of Luke). (See the box "An Archaealogist Looks at Luke.")

Instead of discrediting Luke's account, Ramsay's discoveries kept supporting it. Finally, he concluded that Luke was one of the most accurate historians who had ever written. Influenced by the archaeological evidence, Ramsay became a Christian.

Notice that I say "influenced" by the evidence, not "convinced." I didn't become a Christian because of archaeology, and I wouldn't recommend that anyone else base a faith completely on archaeology, either. Archaeological evidence doesn't *prove* that Jesus is God. What it does do, however, is provide corroborative evidence that the writings about Jesus are trustworthy accounts.

CONTEMPORARY CORROBORATION

At the time that I was investigating the case for Christ, I was a newspaper reporter, not an archaeologist or historian. I know the importance of background research, so I was willing

An Archaeologist Looks at Luke

Several statements in Luke's writings (in the gospel of Luke and the book of Acts) seemed to be inaccurate. And that raised doubts about the rest of what Luke wrote. After all, if he couldn't get the basic facts right, how can you trust his other statements about more important matters?

Then archaeological evidence began coming to light that showed that Luke was in fact correct—at least in those things that archaeologists could check out. Here are a few examples:

In Luke 3:1, Luke refers to Lysanias as tetrarch (that's a kind of regional governing official) of Abilene in about A.D. 27. For years scholars pointed to this as evidence that Luke didn't know what he was talking about, because everybody knew that Lysanias was not a tetrarch but rather the ruler of Chalcis half a century earlier. Then archaeologists found an inscription from A.D. 14 to 37 naming Lysanias as tetrarch in Abila near Damascus—just as Luke had written. It turns out there had been two government officials named Lysanias. Luke was right after all!

Another example is Luke's reference in Acts 17:6 to "politarchs." (If you look it up in the New International Version or other modern translations, you'll see it translated as "city officials.") For a long time people thought Luke was mistaken, because no evidence of the term "politarchs" had been found in any ancient Roman documents. Then archaeologists found a first-century arch (that's the same time period in which Luke was writing) with an inscription that begins, "In the time of the politarchs...." (If you ever get to the British Museum in London, you can see that arch for yourself.) Since then, archaeologists have found more than 35 inscriptions that mention politarchs, showing that Luke was precisely accurate when he used that term.

One prominent archaeologist carefully examined Luke's references to 32 countries, 54 cities, and 9 islands, and didn't find a single mistake.

to take an interest in ancient sources, but my day-to-day focus was on the here and now. I moved in a circle where yesterday's news just didn't make the grade. So I wondered what kind of contemporary/ evidence I might find to back up—or discredit—Christ's claims.

Then I met Ron. I was a *Tribune* reporter covering the criminal courts building, a squat, gloomy facility next to the Cook County jail on Chicago's west side. Day after day I watched a steady stream of defendants—most of them clearly guilty—desperately trying to exploit every loophole to avoid the punishment they deserved. Everybody was looking to cut a deal, to hoodwink the jury, to fool the judge, to beat the rap—anything but take responsibility for what they had done.

Everybody except Ron. He turned everything upside down.

The Book of Mormon

If you find yourself wondering whether archaeology can be used to substantiate the claims of just about any religious belief, you're not alone. I had that same suspicion.

I wrote to the Smithsonian Institute and asked whether any evidence supported the claims of Mormonism and the Book of Mormon. They told me in unequivocal terms that archaeologists see "no direct connection between the archaeology of the New World and the subject matter of the book." As one expert wrote in a book on the topic:

No one has uncovered any of the cities mentioned in the Book of Mormon.

No one has uncovered any artifacts related to the Book of Mormon.

No one has found any inscriptions confirming the Book of Mormon.

No one has identified any person, place, nation, or name mentioned in the Book of Mormon.

Starting Young

When he was 8 years old, Ron threw a hammer at somebody's head and ended up in juvenile court. That was his first of many encounters with the law. Later he dropped out of school, got mixed up with drugs, and rose to second-in-command of the Belaires, a vicious street gang that terrorized parts of Chicago.

He got into big-time trouble when he was 21. A rival gang called the Palmer Street Gaylords brutally assaulted one of Ron's friends, and Ron vowed revenge. He borrowed a gun and went hunting for Bob, who had led the Gaylord attack.

Attempted Murder

It didn't take long for Ron to track down half a dozen Gaylords as they were leaving a bar. Although Bob wasn't among them, his brother Gary was. A plot quickly formed in Ron's mind: he decided to murder Gary, and then when Bob showed up at his funeral, Ron would ambush him too. That way he'd kill *two* Gaylords.

So Ron jumped out of hiding, thrust the gun into Gary's chest, shouted, "Belaires!"—and pulled the trigger.

Click.

The gun misfired. Now Ron was standing in front of 6 very angry Gaylords. As they began to come after him, Ron pointed the gun in the air and pulled the trigger again. This time it went off, sending the Gaylords scattering.

Ron started chasing Gary down the sidewalk, shooting at him as they ran. Finally one of the bullets found its mark, tearing into Gary's back and lodging next to his liver. Gary collapsed face-first on the pavement.

Ron came up to him and flipped him over.

"Don't shoot me, man!" Gary pleaded. "Don't shoot me again! Don't kill me!"

But without an ounce of compassion or a moment of hesitation, Ron shoved the gun in Gary's face and pulled the trigger.

Click!

This time the gun was empty.

On the Run

A siren wailed in the distance. Ron escaped the police, but they promptly issued a warrant for his arrest on a charge of attempted murder. With Ron's extensive criminal record, a conviction would undoubtedly mean 20 years in the penitentiary.

Ron couldn't stomach that. He and his girlfriend fled to Canada, then migrated west and ended up in Portland, Oregon, where Ron got his first legitimate job, working in a metal shop. His coworkers were Christians, and through their influence Ron eventually became a Christian too.

With that his values and character began to change. His girlfriend became a Christian, and they got married. They had a little girl named Olivia. Ron became a model employee, an active church participant, and a well-respected member of the community.

Taking Responsibility

But something kept gnawing at him. Even though he had been reconciled with God, he hadn't been reconciled with society. There was still a warrant out for his arrest. True, the police had stopped looking for him and he probably could have spent the rest of his life in Oregon without getting caught. Still, he felt that the only honest thing to do would be to give himself up and face the possibility of 20 years in prison, away from his family.

Otherwise, he said, he'd be living a lie. And as a Christian, he decided that simply wasn't an option.

Ancient sources say that early Christians clung to their beliefs rather than deny them, even under torture. *Ron* acted on his belief even though he risked 20 years in prison. Why do you think these *people* had such strongly held convictions?

I was there when Ron appeared in criminal court. Amazingly, unlike the other defendants, who were trying to wiggle off the hook, Ron looked into the judge's eyes and basically said, "I'm guilty. I did it. I'm responsible. If I need to go to prison, that's OK. But I've become a Christian, and the right thing to do is to admit what I've done and to ask for forgiveness. What I did was wrong, plain and simple, and I'm sorry. I really am."

I was blown away! When somebody takes a costly step like that, you know it must be prompted by a faith that has radically transformed him or her from deep inside.

And that attracted me. Why? Because we are living in wishy-washy times, when the national motto might as well be, "Take the easy way out." So when someone says, "I'm going to do something not because it's convenient or easy but because it's right," that's a person I can respect. When you look around these days, you don't see many heroes. But in an odd kind of way, Ron became a hero to me.

Radically Changed

I was so intrigued by what Ron did that I asked him about it. When he told me how Jesus had changed him from a street gang leader into a Christ follower, he had my complete attention, and he had a special kind of credibility. Both his example and his words made a lasting impression on me. (And on the judge, too, by the way. He let Ron go free because of the incredible change in Ron's life. Today, Ron is using his freedom to serve young people in a public housing project.)

I had been asking whether there was any evidence outside the Bible that Christ was real and that the Christian faith meant something. Ron's changed life sure looked like that kind of evidence.

But one major question remains for anyone taking seriously the case for Christ: Can a dead man really come back to life?

Jesus and Slavery

One of the ugliest blots on the pages of history is the practice of slavery. Most North Americans, when you mention slavery, think of the enslavement of thousands of African-Americans—some of whom were imported to America as if they were nothing more than cargo, others of whom were born into captivity with little or no hope of ever being free.

But slavery didn't begin on the plantations of North America. The history of slavery goes way, way back—to well before the time of Jesus.

If Jesus is God, and God is ethically perfect, why didn't Jesus put an end to slavery, once and for all, when he lived in Palestine some 2,000 years ago? As far as we know, Jesus never specifically attacked slavery. Why didn't he stand up and shout, "Slavery is wrong"?

When I challenged Donald Carson, a Christian theologian, with this issue, he made the following points:

- First, when we think of slavery today, we think of one race oppressing another race. In Jesus' time, slavery wasn't an issue of race or of class. Some people became slaves during war; others sold themselves into slavery as a way to pay off debts. Slavery—at least among people who respected God—wasn't meant to be life-long, either; the Bible taught that every 7 years all slaves should be set free. Slaves in Jesus' day weren't necessarily abused; some were the equivalent of Ph.D.'s with responsibility for teaching the family. That doesn't mean that slavery was a good thing, but it does mean that it wasn't the destructive racial issue it has been in the U.S.

- Second, you have to keep your eye on Jesus' mission. His primary goal was not to overturn the Roman economic system (which included slavery). After all, one oppressive social system can easily be replaced by another that's even worse. Jesus came to free men and women from their sins. So that was the focus of his message.

- But, what that message does is transform people from the inside, so that they begin to love God and to value other people, too. And that has an impact on what they think of slavery. For example, when the apostle Paul wrote to a Christian named Philemon about Philemon's slave, Onesimus, Paul didn't order Philemon to free his slave. What he did was tell Philemon to treat Onesimus just as he would treat Paul or his own brother. (You can read that letter in the New Testament; it's simply called "Philemon.") And in England and the U.S., it was transformed Christians who successfully campaigned for slavery to be abolished.

Carson speaks as a Christian, so you wouldn't expect him to criticize Jesus for not directly speaking out against slavery.

Whether you find his arguments convincing is something you'll have to decide. What he said about change coming from the inside instead of being forced on people from the outside made sense to me because of my own experience.

I know a guy who was so racist that he disliked anyone who wasn't white. He was particularly prejudiced against African-Americans. The racial slurs he used made me cringe when I was around him, but nothing I said even made a dent in his racism.

Then he became a follower of Jesus. I didn't notice a big difference at first, but gradually the way he talked about people of different races began to change. I noticed other signs that his attitudes were changing, too. If you met him today, you'd have to say that he genuinely accepts people of any race or ethnic background.

Laws against racial profiling didn't change him. Diversity training didn't change him. The disapproval of other people didn't change him. His change came from the inside out, when he realized that the God he followed loves people of all races and calls him to do the same.

CAN A DEAD MAN COME BACK TO LIFE?

three

Did Jesus Fake His Death?

A friend was telling me about Jonathan, a little kid she knows. Jonathan lives on a busy street, and he likes to sit in his front yard and watch the cars and trucks drive by.

One day Jonathan said to his dad, "I know how to make concrete."

"Oh?" replied Jonathan's dad. "How's that?"

"You make it from squirrels," Jonathan said. Noting his dad's look of surprise, he explained. "See, first a squirrel runs into the road. Then it gets hit by a car. Then more cars and more cars drive over it, and in a couple of days, when you look where the squirrel was, it's concrete!"

Jonathan may not have had a very accurate understanding of the composition of concrete or the decomposition of squirrels, but he did get one thing absolutely right: When roadkill disappears, it's not because it came back to life.

Yet Christianity claims that Jesus did exactly that. According to the New Testament, Jesus was "run over" by the force of the Roman government, which authorized the most horrifying form of capital punishment known in that day. His body lay dead for most of three days. Then, according to Christian belief, instead of decomposing, he came back to life.

Christ's resurrection—his coming back to life—is considered the ultimate proof that he is God. So it's too important a claim either to accept mindlessly or to dismiss without looking at it seriously.

Before someone can be resurrected from the dead, of course, the person has to *be* dead. So the first question to ask is, "Did Jesus really die on the cross? Or might he have faked his own death—and the resurrection that appeared to follow?"

STUNNED

There's a family in the Chicago area that likes to visit relatives in Ontario, Canada, every year during Christmas break. Because the weather can be unpredictable and the roads pretty treacherous around the Great Lakes at that time of year, they usually take Amtrak. But almost every trip, it seems, something weird happens to delay their arrival.

One Christmas it was a cow. Zipping along through rural Wisconsin, the passengers suddenly felt a jolt, then a lurch, and then the train shuddered to a squealing halt. When they looked out the window, the family could see train officials and one very angry farmer rushing to the motionless body of a cow. It seems the cow had been on the tracks, and when the train hit it, the cow was thrown clear to where it now lay, half submerged in a snow bank.

Apparently the paperwork involved in a head-on cow collision is significant, because the train sat on the tracks for a long time. When it finally started to move again, the Chicago family went to the end car for one final look at the scene of the accident. The last thing they saw as the train pulled away was the cow, staggering to its feet, twitching a few times, and plodding right back onto the train tracks.

Would you conclude from the evidence that

a) the cow was miraculously raised from the dead, or
b) the cow had been merely stunned and eventually revived?

Option b would be my choice regarding the cow, and, not surprisingly, it used to be a pretty popular choice regarding Jesus' apparent death as well.

RESURRECTED OR REVIVED?

One solution to the problem of a dead person coming back to life is the suggestion that Jesus didn't really die on the cross at all, but that he either fainted from exhaustion or took a drug that made him look dead. Later he revived in the cool, damp air of the tomb. Here are some of the arguments in favor of that theory:

- The Bible itself tells us that Jesus was offered some liquid on a sponge when he was on the cross (see Mark 15:36). If the sponge were drugged, Jesus might appear dead when in fact he was only heavily sedated.
- The Bible also says that Pilate was surprised at how soon Jesus died (Mark 15:44), which could suggest that Jesus was taken off the cross before his crucifixion proved fatal.
- This theory explains how Jesus' tomb could be empty (there was no corpse to bury) and how Jesus could walk and talk and eat with people after his crucifixion.

DEATH BY TORTURE

The other theory, of course, is that Jesus *did* die on the cross. Arguments in favor of that theory include details about just what was involved in the events leading up to the cruci-fixion as well as in crucifixion itself.

Sweating Blood

Luke wrote that when Jesus was praying before he was arrested, "his sweat was like drops of blood" (see Luke 22:44). That sounds like exaggeration at the very least—not the kind of medical accuracy you would hope for from a doctor, which is what Luke was.

But it turns out that doctors today recognize a rare med-ical condition (it's called hematidrosis) that looks like what Luke described. What happens is that high anxiety causes cer-tain chemicals to release into the capillaries in the sweat glands. These chemicals break down the capillaries (very tiny blood vessels) so that there's a small amount of bleeding right in the sweat glands. When the sweat comes out, it's tinged with blood.

Under the Whip

In 1994 an American teenager named Michael Fay made international news when he was convicted of vandalizing cars with spray paint in Singapore. The penalty for his crime was caning. Many Americans had never heard of caning before, but before long anyone who cared to find out had learned that caning is a specific punishment involving striking the offender's bare buttocks with a rattan cane. The process is very consistent: the cane used is 1.2 meters long and 13 millime-ters thick; the person being caned bends over an H-shaped rack, and the caner strikes a blow roughly every 30 seconds.

Like caning in Singapore, flogging in the Roman empire followed a predictable and consistent pattern. The soldier would use a whip of braided leather thongs with metal balls woven into them. When the whip would strike the flesh, these balls would cause deep bruises, which would break open with further blows. And the whip had pieces of sharp bone as well, which would cut into the flesh.

The back of the person being flogged would be so shredded that part of the spine was sometimes exposed by the deep cuts. The lash of the whip would go all the way from the shoulders down to the back, the buttocks, and the back of the legs. The whip would tear into underlying muscles to produce quivering ribbons of bleeding flesh, and sometimes even expose internal organs.

Usually flogging consisted of 39 lashes, although a soldier might inflict more, depending on his mood. Many people died from flogging even before they could be crucified. Those who didn't die often went into shock. (See box: State of Shock.)

By the time the soldiers were done flogging Jesus, he would have been in serious condition—even before the first nail was driven in to hang him on the cross.

State of Shock

A flogging **victim** may go into shock as a result of losing so **much blood**. Four things happen to the body in this state of shock:

- The **heart** races to try to **pump blood** that isn't there;
- Blood **pressure** drops, causing the **victim** to faint or collapse;
- The kidneys stop producing urine to maintain the volume of fluid left in the body;
- The person becomes **very** thirsty as the body craves fluids to replace the lost blood volume.

Jesus showed signs of at least two of these symptoms: when he collapsed while carrying his cross, so that the soldiers ordered Simon of Cyrene to carry it for him, and when he said, "I'm thirsty," while hanging on the cross.

On the Cross

These days when condemned criminals are strapped down and injected with poison, or secured to a wooden chair and subjected to a surge of electricity, the circumstances are highly controlled. Death is so certain that a death-row criminal on the way to the execution chamber is referred to as a "dead man walking."

But how certain was death by the crude, slow, and rather inexact form of execution on a cross? Most people aren't sure just how crucifixion kills its victims. And without a trained medical examiner to officially call the time and cause of death, might Jesus have escaped the experience—brutalized and bleeding, but nevertheless alive?

To answer these questions for myself, I looked into the actual process of crucifixion.

When Jesus arrived at the site where he was to be crucified, he would have been laid down with his arms outstretched on a large beam. The executioner would have taken two sharp spikes, each five to seven inches long, and nailed one through each wrist, into the beam.

Hands or Wrists?

Nearly all the pictures of Jesus on the cross show the nails going through Jesus' palms—probably because the Bible mentions nail marks in Jesus' hands (in John 20:25). But actually, the Romans drove the spikes into their victims wrists (which was considered part of the hand). The bones in the palm aren't strong enough to hold the weight of a human body as it sagged on the cross. The nails would have shredded right through the palms, and the victim would have fallen off the cross.

As the nails pierced the wrists, they would have crushed the large nerve that goes to the hand. If you've ever banged your funny bone, you've experienced what it is to jar a nerve. Imagine taking a pliers and squeezing the nerve in your funny bone, and you have some idea of the pain the spikes in the wrist caused.

For this first step of the process, the horizontal beam was lying on the ground, not yet attached to the vertical beam. At this point Jesus was hoisted as the crossbar was attached to the vertical stake, and then the executioner drove nails through Jesus' feet, crushing and severing the nerves there.

The word *excruciating,* meaning "agonizingly painful,"comes from the word *crucifixion.*

Immediately Jesus' arms would have been stretched by the weight of his body hanging on them—scientists tell us that his arms would have been pulled about six inches longer. Both shoulders would be dislocated by the strain put on them.

The Cause of Death

Severed nerves and dislocated joints don't necessarily kill a person. Once a person is hanging in the vertical position, crucifixion is essentially an agonizingly slow death by asphyxiation.

In order to exhale, the person being crucified must push up on his feet. When he did that, the nails would tear through the feet until they eventually locked up against the ankle bones.

After he managed to exhale, the person would then be able to relax down and take another breath in. Again he'd have to push himself up to exhale, scraping his bloodied back against the rough wood of the cross. This would go on and on until complete exhaustion would take over, and the person wouldn't be able to push up and breathe anymore.

As the person's breathing slowed down, the lack of oxygen would lead to an erratic heartbeat and eventually cardiac arrest.

Water and Blood

The combination of shock, a rapid heart rate, and heart failure result in a collection of clear, watery fluid around the heart and lungs. An incision through the lung and heart would release that fluid as well as blood.

The apostle John described this medical phenomenon in his account of the crucifixion, when he wrote that "one of the soldiers pierced Jesus' side with a spear, bringing a sudden flow of blood and water" (John 19:34).

DEAD OR ALIVE?

Dr. William D. Edwards, writing in the *Journal of the American Medical Association,* drew this conclusion about the crucifixion: "Clearly the weight of the historical and medical evidence indicates that Jesus was dead before the wound to his side was inflicted.... The assumption that Jesus did not die on the cross appears to be at odds with modern medical knowledge."

You can draw your own conclusions. What clinched it for me was this question: Suppose Jesus did survive the cross. Suppose he was able to escape from the burial wrappings, roll the rock away from the tomb, and get past the Roman soldiers who were standing guard. After suffering the trauma of the cross and such catastrophic blood loss, would he have inspired the disciples to hail him as a victorious conqueror of death? Would they have been motivated to start a worldwide movement based on the hope that someday they too would have a post-crucifixion body just like his?

My own conclusion, after weighing the evidence, was to rule out the theory that Jesus didn't really die on the cross. That suggestion no longer seemed plausible. But remember, the central claim of Christianity is not just Jesus' death, but his resurrection. Agreeing that Jesus was dead is still a long way from agreeing that he came back to life.

A Question for the Heart

What could possibly have motivated Jesus to willingly allow himself to be degraded and brutalized the way he was?

What Happened to the Body?

The next time you're having lunch in the school cafeteria, take a look at the milk cartons. Chances are good that one side will feature a photo or a sketch of a missing child with the caption, "Have you seen me?"

It's a sad fact of contemporary life that kids do disappear. Except in the horror movies, however, dead bodies disappear from graves much less frequently. Yet that's exactly what seems to have happened to Christ's body. Christ's empty tomb is, for Christians at least, a symbol of his resurrection. And Christ's resurrection is the ultimate evidence that Jesus is God.

The question you have to answer for yourself is, "Is that empty tomb a sign that Jesus came back to life, or did Jesus become just one more missing person after his death?"

WHO SAYS THE TOMB WAS EMPTY?

I did some research into the beliefs of several skeptic organizations. For some reason, not many atheists deal with the topic of the empty tomb, but I did come across one charge that I had heard before.

Skeptic Jeffrey Jay Lowder said he had trouble believing Christ's tomb was empty because none of the disciples or early Christian preachers pointed to it. He wrote, "We would expect the early Christian preachers to have said: 'You don't believe us? Go look in the tomb yourselves! It's at the corner of Fifth and Main, third sepulcher on the right.'"

Yet, he argued, Peter doesn't mention the empty tomb in his preaching in Acts 2. Lowder concluded, "If even the disciples didn't think the empty tomb tradition was any good, why should we?"

Good question! I checked out that sermon of Peter's, and sure enough, Peter never gives an address for the tomb, and he doesn't use the words "empty tomb" in his sermon.

But it's not quite an open-and-shut case. Peter was certainly implying that the tomb was empty, even if he never used those exact words. Here are some of the references Peter made to Jesus' death and resurrection:

- "With the help of evil people, you put Jesus to death. You nailed him to the cross. But God raised him from the dead. He set him free from the suffering of death. It wasn't possible for death to keep its hold on Jesus" (Acts 2: 23–24, NIrV).
- "Brothers, you can be sure that King David died. He was buried. His tomb is still here today. But David was a prophet.... David saw what was ahead. So he spoke about the Christ rising from the dead. He said that the Christ would not be left in the grave. His body wouldn't rot in the ground. God has raised this same Jesus back to life. We are all witnesses of this" (Acts 2:29–32, NIrV).

Your Call

What do you think? Did Peter believe that Christ's tomb was empty or not? You can read his whole sermon for yourself in Acts 2 to get the full story.

Christians get their view of what happened on Easter Sunday not only from early sermons like Peter's, but also from the accounts in the Gospels (those early biographies of Jesus) and some of the letters sent to early Christian churches. (See the box "Tales of an Empty Tomb.") But what's interesting is that Christians weren't the only ones saying the tomb was empty. The Jewish leaders said so, too! Here's how the arguments went:

> CHRISTIANS: *Jesus' tomb is empty—he's been raised from the dead!*
> JEWISH LEADERS: *No, the disciples must have stolen the body.*

(You can read about this argument in Matthew 28:11–15.)

Now think about it: If Jesus' body were still in the tomb, the argument would have gone something like this:

> CHRISTIANS: *Jesus' tomb is empty—he's been raised from the dead!*
> JEWISH LEADERS: *The tomb isn't empty! That dead body is still in there.*

Despite what I read from critics, it seems that quite a lot of people agreed that Christ's tomb was empty. What they didn't agree on was how it got that way.

GRAVE ROBBERS

The most common way for a dead body to get from one place to another is for someone else to move it. So it's not surprising that the most common theory about how Jesus' body got out of his grave is that someone—or several someones—came and took it. (For another theory, see the box "Sorry—Wrong Sepulchre.") Who? There are different ideas about that.

Disciples in the Dark

The most likely suspects are the disciples. Almost immediately after Jesus' body disappeared, the rumor started circulating that his followers had run off with the corpse.

If you've read any mystery novels or watched any courtroom dramas at all, you know that two crucial considerations in a crime are motive and opportunity. If you want to solve a who-dunnit, you have to find someone who had both a reason to commit the crime (in this case, to steal the body) and the means and chance to do so.

Tales of an Empty Tomb

If you're wondering what the disciples and early Christian teachers believed about what happened to Jesus' body after the crucifixion, you can check out some of these reports.

Biographies

Matthew 27:57—28:15
Mark 16
Luke 24
John 20

Early sermons

Acts 2:22–32
Acts 13:29–37

Letter to a first-century church

1 Corinthians 15:3–4

Did the disciples have a motive to steal Jesus' body? On the surface, it seems possible. The Gospels report that Jesus' followers were stunned, scared, and disillusioned after his death. The followers who had given up hope (read about some of them in Luke 24:13–24) or were hiding in fear behind locked doors (see John 20:19) were maybe not the best candidates for a daring grave robbery, but suppose there were others. If they wanted to spread the story that Jesus had returned to life (even though all they would gain would be persecution), they would definitely need to get rid of that incriminating dead body.

So much for motive. What about opportunity?

Sorry — Wrong Sepulchre

One theory about the empty tomb is that the women who found the tomb empty accidentally went to the wrong grave.

Arguments in favor of the theory:

- Three gospel accounts describe the women reaching an empty tomb and finding someone who says, "You are looking for Jesus of Nazareth. He is not here." (See Matthew 28:1-9; Mark 16:1-8; Luke 24:1-8.)
- The women could have imagined that person was an angel telling them that Jesus was risen, when in fact he was merely a caretaker telling them that Jesus was not in that particular tomb.

Arguments against the theory:

- Those same gospel accounts report that the women were present when Jesus' body was placed in the tomb (Matthew 27:61; Mark 15:47; Luke 23:55). Is it likely that the women would have forgotten where the tomb was? Even if they did, their friend who owned the grave would certainly have known where it was.
- If the women went to the wrong tomb, why didn't the Jewish leaders simply point to the correct tomb, with Jesus' dead body still in it, when the stories of an empty tomb began to circulate?

When I think of grave robbers, I picture Indiana Jones going into some Pharaoh's pyramid, or some bad actor digging up a cemetery in a black-and-white B movie. Those pictures don't fit with the Hallmark version of Jesus' grave that you see on Easter cards, so I decided to find out just what Jesus' tomb was like before I drew any conclusions about whether the disciples had the opportunity to rob it.

Of course, the *Chicago Tribune* wasn't on hand to photograph Jesus' grave at the time of his burial, which is why we have to rely on what archeologists have uncovered (literally) about first-century tombs. As far as they can tell, this is what Jesus grave looked like.

A Piece of the Rock

The tomb was actually like a small room cut out of rock. Instead of a hole in the ground, the way most graves are today, the entrance to this tomb was more like the opening to an above-ground cave. The entrance was low to the ground, though, and there was a slanted groove that led down to it. A large, disk-shaped stone was rolled down this groove and lodged into place across the door. Gravity made it easy to roll the disk down the groove, but it would take several strong people to roll the stone back up to reopen the tomb.

That much we can learn from archeology. The gospel of Matthew agrees with that description and provides some more information.

> As evening approached, a rich man came from the town of Arimathea. His name was Joseph. He had become a follower of Jesus. He went to Pilate and asked for Jesus' body. Pilate ordered that it be given to him.
>
> Joseph took the body and wrapped it in a clean linen cloth. He placed it in his own new tomb that he had cut out of the rock. He rolled a big stone in front of the entrance to the tomb. Then he went away.

The Case for Christ

Mary Magdalene and the other Mary were sitting there across from the tomb.

The next day was the day after Preparation Day. The chief priests and the Pharisees went to Pilate. "Sir," they said, "we remember something that liar said while he was still alive. He claimed, 'After three days I will rise again.' So give the order to make the tomb secure until the third day. If you don't, his disciples might come and steal the body. Then they will tell the people that Jesus has been raised from the dead. This last lie will be worse than the first."

"Take some guards with you," Pilate answered. "Go. Make the tomb as secure as you can." So they went and made the tomb secure. They put a seal on the stone and placed some guards on duty.

Matthew 27:57-66 (NIrV)

SWAC—Sealed with a Cord

To "seal" a tomb in Jesus' day, the authorities would wrap a rope or cord across the entrance. Then they would cover each end of the rope with clay or wax so that no one could move the stone without breaking the seal or cutting the cord. It's possible that the seal included the official imprint of the Roman empire, so anyone who broke the seal would be violating imperial law.

So the New Testament accounts (whose reliability we've already examined in chapters 5 and 6) affirm that there was a seal on Jesus' tomb and that it was guarded by soldiers. Remember those arguments between Christians and Jewish leaders in the years after Jesus death? Let's follow them a little further.

> CHRISTIANS: *Jesus' tomb is empty—he's been raised from the dead!*
> JEWISH LEADERS: *No, the disciples stole the body.*
> CHRISTIANS: *How could they? The guards at the tomb would have stopped them.*

JEWISH LEADERS: Oh, but the guards at the tomb fell asleep.

CHRISTIANS: Right. Trained guards falling asleep on the job—and sleeping through the noise of someone moving the stone. I don't think so. The Jews bribed the guards to say they fell asleep.

If there had been no guards, this argument would not have made any sense. The Jewish leaders would simply have said, "What guards? You're crazy! There were no guards!"

What do you think? Did the disciples have sufficient motive and opportunity to steal Jesus' body from the tomb?

Roman Robbers, Jewish Thieves

Some people, concluding that the disciples didn't have sufficient motive or opportunity to steal Jesus' body, have suggested that the Roman officials or the Jewish leaders smuggled the body out secretly.

Your Call

What do you think? Did the disciples have sufficient motive and opportunity to steal Jesus' body from the tomb?

MOTIVE	OPPORTUNITY
You can't have a dead body lying around in a tomb if you want to say that Jesus came back to life. On the other hand, all the disciples gained by proclaiming the Resurrection was persecution and death.	**Challenges** - The tomb was guarded by soldiers. How could the disciples sneak past them? - The body was enclosed in rock. The noise of trying to remove it surely would have awakened the guards if they had fallen asleep. Incidentally, the guards had a great incentive to stay awake—they risked death if the body was stolen.

The Case for Christ

How Many Days in a Weekend?

Jesus said that he would be buried and rise again in three days. (You can read his claims in Matthew 27:63; Mark 8:31; and John 2:19–21.) But if he was crucified on Good Friday and rose on Easter, he was actually in the grave for two nights, one full day, and parts of two other days. So was Jesus wrong in his predictions? Here's how different people answer that question:

Some critics claim that Jesus was wrong. He said he'd be in the grave for three days, but he wasn't.

A few say that Jesus was actually crucified on Wednesday, not on Friday, which makes three full days in the tomb.

Other scholars assert that, because Jews in Jesus' time referred to any part of a day the same way they referred to a full day, in their terminology Jesus was in the tomb three days—so there is no contradiction.

Certainly the Roman officials, holding the power they did, would have the opportunity. Pilate had ordered the guard; he could easily order them to move the body. And the Jewish leaders seem to have had a lot of Roman cooperation along the way; probably they had sufficient opportunity as well.

But what about motive?

Why would the Romans want to take the body? They sentenced Jesus to death.

Why would the Jewish leaders want to take the body? They wanted Jesus to *stay* dead.

And if they had stolen it, why didn't they simply produce the dead body when the disciples started insisting that Jesus was alive?

WHERE DOES A BODY GO FROM HERE?

The evidence of the Gospels, of the early church, and of the Jewish leaders all points to an empty tomb. That empty tomb could have a natural explanation—like someone's stealing the body—or a supernatural explanation—like Jesus' rising from the dead.

If any of the natural explanations turned out to be true, that would explain one puzzle piece: the disappearance of the body. But it wouldn't explain why the disciples reported Christ's body as resurrected, and it wouldn't explain the radical change in the disciples themselves.

Look at what happened to the disciples: At the time of Jesus' death they were depressed. Peter denied Jesus three

Natural vs. Supernatural

Theologian Bill Craig believes the case for the resurrection is so strong that he was willing to publicly debate an atheist selected by the national spokesman for American Atheists, Inc. Afterward I challenged him on the question of the empty tomb.

I asked, "Even though there are holes in the natural explanations for the empty tomb, aren't they still more believable than the absolutely incredible idea that Jesus was God in the flesh who was raised from the dead?"

Craig responded, "Oh, I don't think so. I think the hypothesis that God raised Jesus from the dead is not at all improbable. In fact, based on the evidence, it's the best explanation for what happened. What is improbable is the hypothesis that Jesus rose *naturally* from the dead. That, I'd definitely agree, is unbelievable."

"Can you make that a little clearer?" I asked.

"What it really comes down to," Craig explained, "is whether the supernatural exists. If it doesn't, then the idea of a dead corpse coming back to life on its own after three days is a pretty lame proposition. But if the supernatural does exist, then it's possible that Jesus was raised by supernatural power."

With that he summarized his position: "As long as the existence of God is even possible, it's possible that he acted in history by raising Jesus from the dead."

How would you respond to Bill Craig?

The Case for Christ

times. The disciples ran away because they were afraid they'd be put to death. They were hiding behind closed doors. John decided he was going back to the family fishing business. But a short time later, these disciples were out boldly proclaiming that Jesus Christ is alive. These once cowardly men were transformed into individuals so certain of what they saw—the resurrected Jesus—that they were willing to go to their death proclaiming that he is the Son of God who came back from the grave. Not only were they *willing* to go to their death, almost all of them—10 out of the 11 remaining disciples—*were* put to death for their faith. Yet none of them gave up their testimony that the resurrection was real and that it authenticated Jesus' claim that he is God.

What happened after the discovery of that empty tomb to change them? That's what chapter 9 explores.

What Did Jesus Do after Easter?

In 1963 the body of 14-year-old Addie Mae Collins, one of four African-American girls tragically murdered in a church bombing by white racists, was buried in Birmingham, Alabama. For years family members kept returning to the grave to pray and leave flowers. In 1998 they decided to move the body to another cemetery.

But when workers went to dig up the body, they returned with a shocking discovery: The grave was empty.

Understandably, family members were terribly upset. Cemetery officials scrambled to figure out what had happened. Several possibilities were raised, the main one being that Addie Mae's tombstone had been erected in the wrong place.

In all of the discussion, however, one explanation was never proposed: Nobody suggested that young Addie Mae had been resurrected to walk the earth again. Why? Because by itself an empty grave does not prove a resurrection.

It's one thing to conclude that Jesus' grave really was empty on Easter Sunday (see chapter 8). While I knew that this was important and necessary evidence for Jesus' resurrection, I was also aware that a missing body is not conclusive proof by itself. If I were going to believe that a dead person came back to life, I'd want more evidence.

SEEING IS BELIEVING

Even the persistent myth that Elvis is still alive wouldn't have gained any momentum without the occasional report of an Elvis sighting. What I needed to know was, were there any Jesus sightings after his death? And if so, were they any more believable than the Elvis sightings reported in those tabloids you find in the checkout lane at Target?

500 EYEWITNESSES

The sighting witnessed by the greatest number of people at one time is reported by the apostle Paul, who wrote this in a letter to the church in Corinth:

> What I received I passed on to you. And it is the most important of all. Here is what it is. Christ died for our sins, just as Scripture said he would. He was buried. He was raised from the dead on the third day, just as Scripture said he would be. He appeared to Peter.
>
> Then he appeared to the Twelve. After that, he appeared to more than 500 believers at the same time. Most of them are still living.

What catches my attention is that last sentence: "Most of them are still living." (You can read it for yourself in 1 Corinthians 15:3–6, NIrV.) Paul either knew some of these people or else he was told by someone who knew them that they were still walking around and willing to be interviewed.

Now stop and think about it: Would you include a statement like that if you weren't absolutely certain that these guys would confirm that they really did see Jesus alive? I mean, Paul was basically inviting people to check it out for themselves. Would he have said this if he wasn't confident they'd back him up?

ATTENTION TO DETAIL

The biographies of Jesus recorded in the Gospels describe Jesus' appearances after his death in great detail (see box: Resurrection Reports), and so do speeches by Peter (see Acts 2) and Paul (Acts 13). Granted, not everyone accepts information that comes from the New Testament but, as we discussed in chapters 5 and 6, I found there are great reasons for trusting the general reliability of the Bible's accounts.

EXAMINING THE ALTERNATIVES

All the evidence in the Gospels and Acts—incident after incident, witness after witness, detail after detail—was extremely impressive. But couldn't there be some plausible alternatives that could explain these apparent encounters with the risen Jesus?

Possibility 1: The Sightings Are Legends

If you've ever gone off on some adventure and come back with stories to tell, you know how those stories can grow bigger and better with each retelling—especially if there were a lot of people involved to add their own variations. The rapids you encountered on a whitewater rafting trip, for example, in memory seem more treacherous, the paddling more heroic, and your tumble out of the raft positively death-defying.

Maybe that's how the reports of Jesus' resurrection appearances got going. Maybe the accounts are merely legends that grew up over time.

Resurrection Reports

You can read these reports of Jesus sightings for yourself. Do they have the ring of truth to you? How would you evaluate them as evidence for Jesus' resurrection?

Appearance to Mary Magdalene, in John 20:10–18;

To other women, in Matthew 28:8–10;

To Cleopas and another traveler on the road to Emmaus, in Luke 24:13–32;

To 11 disciples and others, in Luke 24:33–49;

To 10 apostles and others, with Thomas absent, in John 20:19–23;

To Thomas and the other apostles, in John 20:26–30;

To 7 apostles, in John 21:1–14;

To the disciples, in Matthew 28:16–20.

And he was with the apostles at the Mount of Olives, in Luke 24:50–52 and Acts 1:4–9.

One argument in favor of this possibility is the fact that the accounts become more numerous throughout the Gospels: Mark records no appearances; Matthew has some; Luke has more; and John has the most.

People who don't agree that the reports are merely legends offer the following arguments:

- Legends take a story and make it bigger, but they don't tell you how the story got started in the first place. *Something* happened to make the apostles believe that Jesus rose from the grave and to make the resurrection the central teaching of the earliest church.

- The biggest claim about eyewitnesses—the report in 1 Corinthians 15 that mentions Jesus' appearing to 500 people—was circulating *before* the earliest Gospels were written. (Paul wrote and sent many letters that are part of the New Testament, including 1 Corinthians, before the Gospels were written down.) That's the opposite of how a legend works, which starts small and grows. Also, the 1 Corinthians 15 report comes so soon after the resurrection that historians say there wasn't anywhere near enough time for legend to grow up and wipe out a solid core of truth.

- What about the empty tomb? If the resurrection were merely a legend, there would have to be another hypothesis to explain why there was no body in the grave on Easter morning.

Possibility 2: The Sightings Were Hallucinations

Maybe the witnesses were sincere in believing they saw Jesus. Perhaps they accurately reported what they saw. But could they have been seeing a hallucination that convinced them they were encountering Jesus when they really weren't?

The biggest argument in favor of the hallucination theory, as far as I'm concerned, is that hallucinations are more common than resurrections. It's generally easier to believe that someone is hallucinating than that someone came back to life.

But I talked to experts on hallucinations who make these points:

- Hallucinations happen to individuals. Only one person can see a hallucination at a time; a group of people, whether there are 10, 12, or 500 of them, would not have the same hallucination at the same time.
- Hallucinations may be more common than resurrections, but they are still relatively rare. Most hallucinations are caused by drugs or by going without food, water, or sleep. The odds that hundreds of people from many different situations suddenly began having hallucinations over the same period of time are incredibly low.
- If people only *thought* they saw Jesus, his body would still be in the grave.

Possibility 3: Wishful Thinking

You probably know people who almost always manage to see what they want to see, to spin a situation to suit what they already believe. Like the guy who's convinced he's God's gift to women: a girl can walk past him without so much as a glance in his direction, and he'll turn to you and say, "She wants me!" Or the group that thinks their band is on the verge of breaking into the big time, even though they've never gotten a gig outside their own garage.

Maybe Jesus' followers were so set on seeing Jesus rise from the grave that they talked themselves—and one another—into believing it had happened. People who accept this possibility will tell you that stranger things have happened in the name of faith.

People who don't accept the "wishful thinking" argument will tell you:

- The early Christians had too much at stake to make a delusion the center of their belief system. They were willing to go to their deaths defending the truth of the resurrection. Wouldn't you expect them to quietly give up the belief when it became an issue of getting killed?
- This theory depends on the tendency many people have to believe what they want to believe. But two of the eyewitnesses, at least, didn't *want* to believe that Jesus came back to life at all! James was skeptical of Jesus during his lifetime, and Paul actively persecuted Christians. How did they get talked into this delusion?
- And, again, this theory doesn't explain the problem of the empty tomb.

CLOSE ENCOUNTERS

If you're into logic, or history, or theology, you probably find all these lists of eyewitnesses and arguments for and against Christ's resurrection pretty gripping.

But if you're not into any of those things, you may be wondering, "What difference does it really make whether Jesus showed up and proved he was alive to a bunch of people who are now dead themselves?"

And that's a good question.

Because if Jesus' resurrection doesn't have anything to do with life today, does it matter whether he rose from the dead or not?

Encounters with Jesus 2,000 years ago may be the stuff of theology, but encounters with Jesus today—now that could make me sit up and take notice! And that's exactly what a professor named J.P. Moreland claims to have experienced.

We were bantering about football and whether his team (the Kansas City Chiefs) or mine (the Chicago Bears) had any

Faithful or Fanatic?

One argument I heard several times as I investigated the claims of Christianity had to do with the passion of the early believers. Christianity must be true, the argument went, because the disciples were willing to die for it. (See the box "You Lie, You Die," in chapter 5.)

"Yes," I would agree, "they were willing to die for their beliefs. But so are Muslims and Mormons and followers of Jim Jones and David Koresh. This may show that they were fanatical, but let's face it: it doesn't prove that what they believed is true."

Then one day someone put it to me this way: People will die for their religious beliefs if they sincerely believe they're true, but people won't die for their religious beliefs if they know their beliefs are false.

Most people have only their faith to tell them that their beliefs are true. Muslims, for example, believe that Allah revealed himself to Muhammad. But this revelation didn't happen in a public way that anyone could observe. So they could be wrong—and they have no way to verify it one way or the other. But if they sincerely *believe* it's true, they might be willing to die for those beliefs if called upon to do so.

The disciples, on the other hand, were in a position to know without a doubt whether Jesus had risen from the dead. They claimed that they saw him, talked with him, and ate with him. If none of that really happened, then regardless of what they may have told others, the disciples themselves would know that the rapidly spreading belief in Jesus' resurrection was all a hoax, born of their own untrue statements. Certainly they wouldn't have let themselves be tortured to death for what they knew to be untrue.

chance of making it to the Super Bowl (probably not) when Moreland casually mentioned, "You've forgotten a whole category of encounters with Christ, you know."

After taking a second or two to shift gears from football to evidence for Christ's resurrection, I finally said, "I give up. What encounters do you mean?"

"It's the ongoing encounter with the resurrected Christ that happens all over the world, in every culture, to people from all kinds of backgrounds and personalities," he said. "They all will tell you that more than any single thing in their lives, Jesus Christ has changed them."

Moreland leaned forward for emphasis. "To me, this is the final evidence—not the only evidence, but the final confirming proof—that the message of Jesus can open the door to a direct encounter with the risen Christ."

"I assume you've had an encounter like that," I said. "Tell me about it."

"I was a cynical chemistry major at the University of Missouri when I was confronted with the fact that if I examined the claims of Jesus Christ critically but with an open mind, there was more than enough evidence for me to believe it.

"So I took a step of faith in the same direction the evidence was pointing, by receiving Jesus as my forgiver and leader. And I began to relate to him—to the resurrected Christ—in a very real and ongoing way.

"In three decades since then, I've had hundreds of specific answers to prayer, I've had things happen that simply cannot be explained by natural explanations, and I have experienced a changed life beyond anything I could have imagined."

"Wait a minute," I protested. "Lots of people in other religions experience life change, too. Isn't it dangerous to base a decision on an experience you can't prove?"

The Case for Christ

The Resurrection of Debbie

In 1995, Debbie Habermas slowly, painfully died of stomach cancer. A few years later her husband, Gary, who's a leading expert on Jesus' resurrection, told me this story.

"I sat on our porch," he began, gazing off at nothing in particular. "My wife was upstairs dying. Except for a few weeks, she was home through it all. It was an awful time. This was the worst thing that could possibly happen.

"I knew if God were to come to me, I'd ask only one question. 'Lord, why is Debbie up there in bed, dying?' And I think God would respond by asking gently, 'Gary, did I raise my Son from the dead?'

"I'd say, 'Come on, Lord! I've written several books on that topic! Of course he was raised from the dead! But I want to know about Debbie!'

"I think he'd keep coming back to the same question—'Did I raise my Son from the dead?' 'Did I raise my Son from the dead?'—until I got his point: the resurrection says that if Jesus was raised 2,000 years ago, there's an answer to Debbie's death in 1995. And do you know what? It worked for me while I was sitting on the porch, and it still works today.

"It was a horribly emotional time for me, but I couldn't get around the fact that the resurrection is the answer for her suffering. I still worried; I still wondered what I'd do raising four kids alone. But there wasn't a time when that truth didn't comfort me.

"Losing my wife was the most painful experience I've ever had to face, but if the resurrection could get me through that, it can get me through anything. It was good for 30 A.D., it's good for 2000, and it's good beyond that."

Gary locked eyes with mine. "That's not some sermon," he said quietly. "I believe that with all my heart. If there's a resurrection, there's a heaven. If Jesus was raised, Debbie will be raised. And I will be someday, too.

"Then I'll see them both."

"Let me make two things clear," Moreland said. "First, I'm not saying, 'Just trust your experience.' I'm saying, 'Use your mind calmly and weigh the evidence, and then see whether your experience confirms that evidence.' Second, if what this evidence points to is true, the evidence itself begs for an experiential test."

"An experiential test?" I repeated. "Define that."

"The experiential test is, 'He's alive, and I can find out by relating to him.' If you were on a jury and heard enough evidence to convince you of someone's guilt, it wouldn't make sense to stop short of the final step of convicting him. And for people to accept the evidence for the resurrection of Jesus and not take the final step of testing it experientially would be to miss where the evidence is leading."

Which, of course, leads to the obvious question: are you open to taking that step?

Conclusion: So What?

When you read about somebody else's struggle with questions about God and faith and life, the process can seem fairly straightforward and orderly. In real life, it isn't always so clear. I sorted through the evidence for and against Christ for a year and 9 months, sometimes jumping from one issue to another and then back again. Finally, I realized it was time to deal with the most pressing question of all: "So what?"

FROM KNOWLEDGE TO EXPERIENCE

I remember one afternoon when I was 14 years old. I was home by myself, painting with oil colors on a large canvas in the basement. While acrylics dry fairly quickly, oil paints seem to take forever. Growing impatient, I plugged in a couple of heat lamps to hurry matters along.

Not smart.

A short time later a pile of rags soaked in turpentine went up in flames. Then the table started on fire, and soon the entire corner of the wood-paneled basement was ablaze.

If...	Then...
Jesus is the Son of God...	his teachings are more than just good ideas from a wise teacher; they are God's own insights—on which I can confidently build my life.
Jesus sets the standard for morality...	I can have an unchanging foundation for my choices and decisions, rather than basing them on the changing values of what seems to get me ahead in a particular situation.
Jesus did rise from the dead...	he's still alive today and available for me to encounter on a personal basis.
Jesus conquered death...	he can open the door of eternal life for me, too.
Jesus has divine power...	he has the supernatural ability to guide me and transform me as I follow him.
Jesus personally knows the pain of loss and suffering...	he can comfort and encourage me when things go wrong.
Jesus loves me as he says...	he has my best interests at heart. That means I have nothing to lose and everything to gain by committing myself to him.
Jesus is who he claims to be...	as my Creator he deserves my obedience and worship.

The Case for Christ

I ran to the telephone to call the fire department. When I returned, I saw that the fire was out of control, with orange and yellow flames lapping the ceiling, which was directly beneath the living room. I knew that if the fire burned through, the whole house would be consumed—and then I'd *really* be in trouble.

I grabbed a bucket of water from the laundry room, dashed over to the fire, and threw it on the wall where the flames were climbing. That didn't even slow the fire down. The basement was quickly filling with a thick, black, sooty smoke. And then the lights shorted out.

Choking on the smoke and fumes, I was quickly becoming disoriented. I couldn't see the stairs anymore. That's when a horrible realization hit—I couldn't save myself. I wouldn't be able to find the way out of the basement before I was overcome. I was in a life-threatening situation.

Just then a police officer arrived and opened the door to the basement. He stepped onto the top stair and began shining around a big flashlight. "Police officer!" he called out. "Anybody down there?"

I could have analyzed the situation intellectually. Things were serious in the basement; if I stayed down there much longer, chances were that I would die from the smoke and fire. But the police officer knew the only escape route. He was a trained professional and fully capable of leading me to safety. What's more, he held a big flashlight to illuminate the way for me.

I grasped and understood all of that without even stopping to think about it. But it wasn't enough just to understand it. I had to take a step of action. I had to put my faith in that officer—a faith based on facts—by letting him reach out and rescue me. So I followed the light, and he put his arm around me and led me to safety, away from the fire.

After nearly 2 years of investigating the claims of Jesus, I knew he had unique credentials and credibility. And based on what he said, I realized that I couldn't save myself.

And yet just knowing that wasn't enough. I needed more than just an intellectual decision. I had to act on it by letting him put his arm around me and lead me to safety. I had to take the experiential step that J. P. Moreland had described (see chapter 9).

So **What?**

But I no longer felt as if I were trying to swim upstream against the strong current of evidence; instead I was going in the same direction that the facts seemed to be flowing. That felt reasonable. It also felt, in some way I can't really explain, like what I sensed God's Spirit nudging me to do.

So on November 8, 1981, I talked with God from the heart. I admitted my wrongdoing and I received the gift of forgiveness and eternal life through Jesus. I told him that with his help I wanted to follow him and his ways from here on out.

There were no lightning bolts, no audible replies, no tingly sensations. Some people feel a rush of emotion at such a moment; I didn't. But I knew that what had happened was real.

SOMETHING NEW

The apostle Paul wrote, "Anyone who believes in Christ is a new creation. The old is gone! The new has come!" (2 Corinthians 5:17, NIrV) And sure enough, over time as I tried to follow Jesus' teachings and open myself to his power, I began to change. Jesus gave me a moral compass to live my life by, so I wasn't hurting people in the ways I used to, or hurting myself. He took away the tremendous fear I had of dying, because he conquered death. He relieved the guilt that had weighed me down. He gave a new dimension to my relationships. He revitalized my family.

Jesus has given me encouragement when I've needed it and direction when I've asked for it. He's given a meaning to my life that goes far beyond just me.

REACHING YOUR OWN VERDICT

So what about you? You've heard my experience, but your own conclusion is up to you. No one can make up your mind for you.

Maybe, after exploring the issues and the evidence, you've decided, as I did, that the case for Christ is conclusive. What's next? If you want to experience Christ for yourself, all you need is to receive Jesus' grace. You can do that by talking to him from your heart, admitting the things you've done wrong, and accepting Jesus as your forgiver and leader. You'll become his son or daughter, and you'll be launched on a spiritual adventure that will continue for the rest of your life—and into eternity.

The Case for Christ

if you are ...	Then try reading ...
• practical • a nuts-and-bolts type of person • mathematically or scientifically inclined	The gospel of Luke, for its clarity and detail.
• artistic • poetic • a philosophical thinker	the gospel of John, for its poetry and powerful imagery.
• from a Jewish background	the gospel of Matthew, for its treatment of prophecies about the Messiah.

But maybe you still have questions. Then keep searching. One of the best things you can do is to read the Bible for yourself. (You might like to try *The Journey,* which is an edition of the Bible for people who aren't yet sure that it's the word of God.)

You might even think about asking God for help. After all, what's to lose? If nobody's really there in heaven, all you've lost is a few seconds. But if God is real and he is listening—well, you could be a winner in a big way.

Here's the prayer I prayed when I started my own investigation into the case for Christ.

God, I don't even believe you're there, but if you are, I want to find you. I really do want to know the truth. So if you exist, please show yourself to me.

You can use this or one of your own. But brace yourself: You may get what you ask for. I did.

ABOUT THE AUTHOR

Lee Strobel, who holds a Master of Studies in Law degree from Yale Law School, as well as a journalism degree from the University of Missouri, is the former legal editor of the *Chicago Tribune*. His awards include Illinois' highest honors for both investigative reporting and community service journalism from United Press International. His journey from atheism to Christianity was documented in his Gold Medallion–winning bestseller, *The Case for Christ: A Journalist's Personal Investigation of the Evidence for Jesus.*

Currently, Lee is a teaching pastor at Saddleback Valley Community Church in Lake Forest, California, and is a board member of the Willow Creek Association. Previously, Lee was a teaching pastor at Willow Creek Community Church in suburban Chicago, and he has taught First Amendment law at Roosevelt University.

His other bestsellers include *Inside the Mind of Unchurched Harry and Mary,* which also won a Gold Medallion, *What Jesus Would Say,* and *God's Outrageous Claims,* all published by Zondervan. His book *Reckless Homicide* has been used as a supplementary text at several law schools.

Lee and his wife, Leslie, have been married for twenty-eight years and have two adult children: Alison, an elementary education graduate of the University of Illinois, and Kyle, a biblical studies graduate of Judson College.

If you want to go **deeper** into the topics Lee introduced, get the complete story.

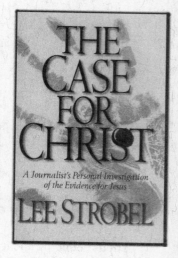

The Case for Faith
A Journalist Investigates the Toughest Objections to Christianity

In his bestseller *The Case for Christ,* Lee Strobel examined the claims of Christ, reaching the hard-won yet satisfying verdict that Jesus is God's unique son.

But despite the compelling historical evidence that Strobel presented, many grapple with doubts or serious concerns about faith in God. As in a court of law, they want to shout, "Objection!" They say, "If God is love, then what about all of the suffering that festers in our world?" Or, "If Jesus is the door to heaven, then what about the millions who have never heard of him?"

In *The Case for Faith,* Strobel turns his tenacious investigative skills to the most persistent emotional objections to belief, the eight "heart" barriers to faith. *The Case for Faith* is for those who may be feeling attracted toward Jesus, but who are faced with formidable intellectual barriers standing squarely in their path. For Christians, it will deepen their convictions and give them fresh confidence in discussing Christianity with even their most skeptical friends.

Hardcover 0-310-22015-7
Softcover 0-310-23469-7
Evangelism Pack 0-310-23508-1
Mass Market 6-pack 0-310-23509X
Audio Pages® Abridged Cassettes 0-310-23475-1

Pick up a copy at your favorite bookstore today!

> *"My road to atheism was paved by science. . . .*
> *But, ironically, so was my later journey to God."*—
> Lee Strobel

The Case for a Creator:

A Journalist Investigates Scientific Evidence That Points Toward God

Lee Strobel, Author of
The Case for Christ *and*
The Case for Faith

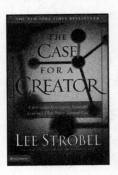

During his academic years, Lee Strobel became convinced that God was outmoded, a belief that colored his ensuing career as an award-winning journalist at the *Chicago Tribune*. Science had made the idea of a Creator irrelevant—or so Strobel thought.

But today science is pointing in a different direction. In recent years, a diverse and impressive body of research has increasingly supported the conclusion that the universe was intelligently designed. At the same time, Darwinism has faltered in the face of concrete facts and hard reason.

Has science discovered God? At the very least, it's giving faith an immense boost as new findings emerge about the incredible complexity of our universe. Join Strobel as he reexamines the theories that once led him away from God. Through his compelling and highly readable account, you'll encounter the mind-stretching discoveries from cosmology, cellular biology, DNA research, astronomy, physics, and human consciousness that present astonishing evidence in *The Case for a Creator*.

Hardcover: 0-310-24144-8
Unabridged Audio Pages® CD: 0-310-25439-6
ebooks:
Adobe Acrobat eBook Reader®: 0-310-25977-0
Microsoft Reader®: 0-310-25978-9
Palm™ Edition: 0-310-25979-7
Unabridged ebook Download: 0-310-26142-2

The Case for a Creator— Student Edition

A Journalist Investigates Scientific Evidence That Points Toward God

Lee Strobel with Jane Vogel

In *The Case for a Creator—Student Edition*, bestselling author and former atheist Lee Strobel and popular writer Jane Vogel take younger readers on a remarkable investigation into the origin of the universe, interviewing many of the world's most renown scientists and following the evidence wherever it leads.

Their findings—presented in the third blockbuster "Case" book student edition—offer the most compelling scientific proof ever for intelligent design. Perfect for youth groups and young people eager to rebut the Darwinian and naturalistic views taught so commonly in schools.

Softcover: 0-310-24977-5

Pick up a copy today at your favorite bookstore!